An Economics Primer
Foundations for the Study of Economics

Mark A. Selzer
Ian R. Gibson

For Paul & Kay, for Derek & Joan

An Economics Primer:
Foundations for the Study of Economics

Mark A. Selzer; Associate Professor; Inter-faculty Institute for International Studies, Ritsumeikan University, Japan

Ian R. Gibson; Associate Professor; Inter-faculty Institute for International Studies, Ritsumeikan University, Japan

ISBN-10: 061532259X
ISBN-13: 978-0-615-32259-9
Copyright © 2009
MIB Publications
California, USA

Table of Contents

Preface

Who will find this book useful?

This book was written with the purpose of providing readers with little prior study or knowledge of economics with a basic preliminary understanding of some of the concepts upon which this social science is based. This book does not seek to provide a comprehensive survey of the field but rather to help students prepare for future study of a more ambitious nature.

Just as if you decided to join your school's track team for the first time, you might feel that you should start an exercise program a few months before the season begins. This preparation will help you to make the best possible start, and perhaps allow you to qualify for a spot in your most favored events.

This analogy illustrates the spirit in which this book should be used. Understanding economic concepts often depends on an adequate understanding of the prior concepts on which subsequent concepts rest. This book tries to present the most basic economic concepts in easy-to-understand descriptions, in order to offer the best possible preparation for future study of microeconomics, macroeconomics, and international economics. Furthermore, the authors would contend that understanding these basic economic concepts is not only important for those planning further study, but also important for all consumers regardless of academic interest.

SECTION ONE

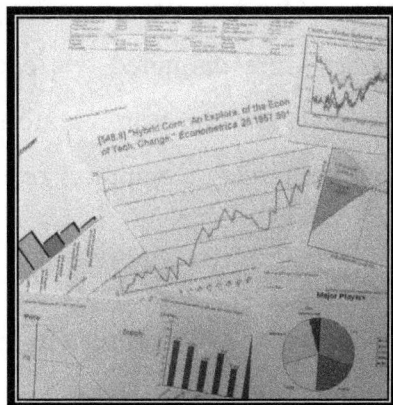

Foundational Concepts for Understanding Basic Economics

Defining Economics

There are several ways in which one can define economics. Economics is often misunderstood as the study of money and business. This definition is far too narrow. Economics is the science of choice. It is the study of how people, businesses, and societies choose to allocate their time, money, energy and all other resources. This study of economics is the study of how these choices are made, the consequences of these choices, and how to improve the quality of our choices in the future.

Unlike the physical sciences, which focus on the phenomena in the physical or natural world, economics is a *social science*, which focuses on elements of the behavior of human social relations. Economics can be more specifically defined as the social science concerned with how limited resources are used to satisfy people's unlimited wants and needs. To better understand this definition we will now discuss what we mean when we speak of *resources* as well as *wants* and *needs.*

We use the term **resources** to describe the *factors,* or inputs, that are used in the production of goods and services. The first and most important thing to understand about resources is that nearly every resource of any type has a limited supply. If the supply of all resources were unlimited, we could then produce an unlimited supply of any goods or services that we want. Unfortunately we all know that is only so much gold, oil, workers, money, computers or time available at any given time to make anything.

Do you have everything you want?   Unfortunately, most of us do not. Therefore, unlike resources, our wants and needs are *unlimited.* **Needs** could be described as something we require for daily life. Food, energy, and medicine are all typical examples of goods that one might consider necessary to their livelihood. **Wants** could be described as goods or services that individuals might believe could improve the quality of their lives, but could be done without, if necessary.   An economic term often used to refer to wants and needs is called *demand.*

In summary then, resources are limited but our wants and needs (or *demand*) is unlimited. This brings is to the economic concept of *scarcity.*

The Concept of Scarcity

Previously in this section we mentioned that economics is the science of choice. Decisions about what goods and services to produce and how to produce them involve **scarcity** -- which assesses the limited resources for production relative to the demand for goods and services.

All economic systems depend on resources, natural and manufactured for the success of the economy. Given that resources are finite, i.e. limited and therefore scarce, systems have to make choices (discussed further in Section 2) as how best to utilize these precious resources.

It is important that you do not confuse the economic concept of scarcity with its common dictionary synonym of *rarity*. If something is rare, it is merely uncommon. However, in economic terminology, something is **scarce** if: 1) it has a cost; and 2) people want or need it (or rather, there is a *demand* for it). The higher the cost and the greater the demand there is for something; then the greater the scarcity of that particular thing.

Two related terms that are sometimes used to describe goods are related to the idea of scarcity. An **economic good** refers to any good or service that sells for a price; that is, a good that is not free. It has a cost and therefore if there is a demand for it, then it is also scarce.

The opposite of an economic good would be a **free good** -- a production or consumption good that does not have a direct cost (and is therefore not scarce).

Economic Reasoning Questions 1.1

1. What two factors make a good scarce?

a. _____

b. _____

2. A good that has a direct cost is a(n) _____ good and a good that has no direct cost is a(n) _____ good.

3. Write an "S" next to each of the following items that are scarce.

a. _____ Drinking water

b. _____ Weeds

c. _____ Clean air

d. _____ Influenza virus

e. _____ Time

f. _____ Money

g. _____ Toxic Waste

h. _____ Teachers

Resources and Production

The various types of resources we use to produce goods are often referred to as the *factors of production*. The **factors of production** can include natural resources, human resources, and capital resources, in addition to the financial capital used to purchase all other resources, and the entrepreneurial resources necessary to combine all other resources in order to produce a new good or service.

Natural resources, or sometimes referred to as **land resources,** includes all "gifts of nature" including mineral deposits like gold or oil, forest resources like timber or rubber, oceanic resources like fisheries, or any other natural process that contributes to production including rain or sunshine.

Human resources, or sometimes referred to as **labor resources,** includes all production resources performed by human beings, including manual work (done by hand), clerical (office) tasks, technical work (such as computer programming), professional work (like a doctor or a lawyer), and managerial labor.

A third factor of production is often referred to as **capital resources**, or **physical capital**. It is important not to confuse this term with the similarly worded term **financial capital**.

Capital resources refers to the means of production, including computers, robots, factories, office buildings, machines, tools, desks, chairs, and other equipment. Capital resources also include **technology** and information such as software or trade secrets.

Financial capital is not really a resource; but it provides the means for businesses or entrepreneurs to buy the various factors of production they need to produce a particular product. Simply put, financial capital is the money to acquire the main factors of production -- the land, labor, and capital resources necessary for production of a product.

A final concept related to the factors of production is *entrepreneurship*. An **entrepreneur** is a business innovator who sees the opportunity to make a profit from a new product or new process, and then brings together the land, labor, and capital resources in order to profit from the opportunity.

While entrepreneurship is surely essential to the factors of production, for our introductory purposes, we will primarily focus on land, labor, and capital when discussing resources for production.

Economic Reasoning Questions 1.2

1. Which category does each of the following resources belong? Write "land", "labor" or "capital" next to each.

a. Oil _____

b. Secretary _____

c. Computer Chip Factory _____

d. Water _____

e. Technology _____

f. Taxi Driver _____

g. Office Building _____

h. Farmland _____

2. Think of an occupation (student, doctor, lawyer, housewife, etc.) and think of five different resources that performing the occupation requires.

Occupation: _____

Resources: (land, labor and capital)

a. _____

b. _____

c. _____

d. _____

e. _____

The Scientific Method

All sciences make use of the *scientific method*, whether they are physical sciences like chemistry or social sciences like psychology. **Scientific method** is a procedure used by scientists to develop explanations for events and test the validity of those explanations. Almost 200 years ago, Charles Darwin made meticulous use of the scientific method to develop his theories of evolution.

As mentioned earlier, economics is a social science that focuses on patterns of human behavior, specifically those choices involving the use of resources to satisfy demand. Like any other science, economics makes use of the scientific method as well. Unfortunately, unlike other sciences, economics is difficult to test under controlled laboratory conditions. Nevertheless, the scientific method still provides a helpful methodology for the study of economic relationships. For economists, the world is their laboratory.

Steps of the Scientific Method

Step 1: Observe an event under certain conditions.

Step 2: Create a *hypothesis* as to why that event occurred.

A **hypothesis** is a tentative explanation of an event; used as a basis for further research.

Step 3: Test the hypothesis

This might include gathering additional information or performing experiments. The goal of such an experiment will attempt to recreate the same result under the same conditions of the original observation. The results of the experiment should either suggest that your hypothesis is correct, incorrect, or maybe just in need of adjustment.

Step 4: Tentatively accept, revise, or reject the hypothesis.

Ultimately the quality of a hypothesis is its ability to predict future events. Therefore if the conditions assumed by the hypothesis leads to the same experimental result, you may then accept the hypothesis as accurate, or *valid*. If the experimental result is different under the same conditions, you may then reject your hypothesis as inaccurate, or *invalid*. If your experimental results are close to the predicted result, you might choose to adjust, or revise, your hypothesis and test it again.

Economic Reasoning Questions 1.3

1. List the steps of the scientific method for the following example.

a. You notice that many of your classmates who study hard get good scores on their exams.

_____

b. You theorize that students who attend more classes get higher scores.

_____

c. You administer an anonymous survey asking students their number of absences and their exam scores for the class.

_____

d. You compare the numbers and discover that there is a connection between the numbers but not as strong as you expected.

_____

e. You adjust your hypothesis to include attendance AND hours reading the textbook for each class.

_____

f. You administer a second survey that includes a question asking how many hours students spend reading the textbook.

_____

g. You notice that nearly all students who regularly attend class and spend several hours reading the textbook get higher test scores.

_____

h. You conclude that good attendance and completing ones reading assignment will lead to good test scores.

_____

What is Economic Reasoning?

Economic reasoning is the term given to describe the way an economist thinks about things. You might define **economic reasoning** as the application of the tools of economic analysis to explain economic developments or to solve economic problems. Economic reasoning is similar to critical thinking. It makes use of logical analysis, but must also take value judgments into account. The next section will focus on the tools of economic reasoning.

The Tools of Economic Reasoning

Economists use different sets of tools to apply economic reasoning to explain an economic development or to solve an economic problem. Some of these tools involve analysis of factual information and some of these tools involve theoretical applications.

The **factual tools** used by economists are historical observation, institutional behavior, and statistical analysis.

Economic **history** helps economists understand past patterns and how to use that information to deal with current problems. Since controlled laboratory experiments are not available to study the relationships of society's economic behavior, the actual events of past economic activities can be very useful for finding patterns and relationships between variables under conditions that might be re-created in the future.

Institutions are decision-making units, established practices, or laws. They are organizations, customs or patterns of behavior in a society. For example, some of our labor decisions about how to decide what jobs people can do are decided by society's institutions. In many societies, more women become medical nurses than men. The reason for this has far less to do with the innate abilities of men and women for this job, than the fact that nursing has *customarily* been an occupation held by women.

In many countries, a person wanting to teach courses at the college or university-level would have to have a minimum of a masters-level graduate training to qualify. In most cases this is not due to any government requirement, but rather this is the agreed upon *established practice* of all of the employers in the particular industry (in this case, college and university leaders have a consensus agreement about minimum requirements for instructors at this level of education).

If a person wanted to become a medical doctor, most countries have laws requiring not only a minimum level of education, but also that all doctors have some kind of license to practice medicine. This decision on who can be a doctor is a matter of law.

Statistics are often needed for understanding a problem and deciding what to do about it. **Statistics** are the data that describe economic *variables*, or numbers with changeable values. Statistics also refers to the techniques of analyzing, interpreting, and presenting data. Powerful mathematical techniques are available to help economists analyze the relationship, or *correlation*, between different measurements of economic variables.

A **direct relationship** is defined as a relationship between two *variables* in which their values increase and decrease together. For example, if you look at two data variables such as height and weight in a large group of individuals, you might notice that as average height increases, the average weight increases as well. This does not mean that a single individual can predict his or her own weight based on this observation, but one can surmise that on average there is a direct relationship between height and weight.

Figure 1.1   **Figure 1.2**

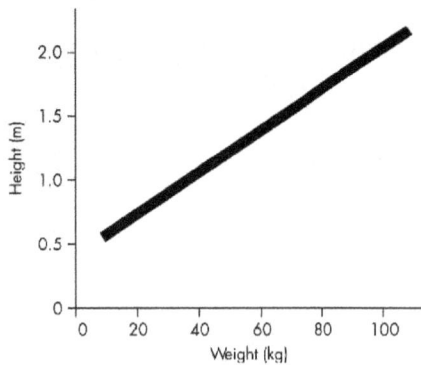

Hypothetical relationship between
height and weight in a population

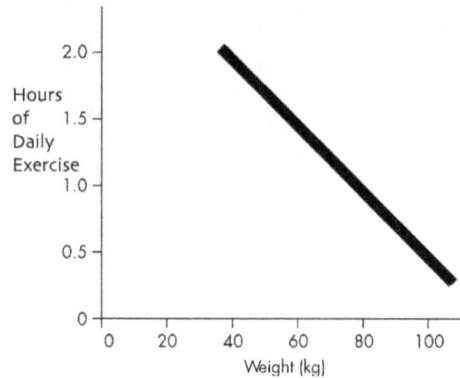

Hypothetical relationship between
weight and exercise in a population

You might notice a different relationship between the variables of weight and number of hours spent per week exercising. Data will likely show that as the *average number of hours exercising goes up, average weight will go down.* This would be an example of an **inverse relationship** -- a relationship between two variables in which the value of one decreases as the value of the other increases.

Statistical analysis also includes the interpretation of these correlations, or what significance the connections of these related measurements might hold. A final important element of statistics is the presentation of the data in ways that the possible relationships between variables are more understandable to others.

Graphs are useful to present data to others to make the relationships you are discussing more understandable. Is also important for all of us to be able to read and interpret (or perhaps critique) graphs for the information that they display. Graphs are quite commonplace in our everyday lives -- in the news media and in many of today's common occupations.

Visual Models: Using Charts and Graphs

There are many types of descriptive charts that are graphical representations of statistical data or other information. A *pie chart* is useful for showing shows the relative size of the components (parts) of a whole. A *line graph* displays how two variables relate to each other. One specific type of line graph is called a *time series* that graphs the changes in the values of a variable over time. In these graphs, time (usually years) is one of the variables. Column charts, bar charts (like column charts on their side) and area charts are useful for displaying changes in multiple variables over time. Following are examples of each type.

Pie Chart

Avererage Student Scores

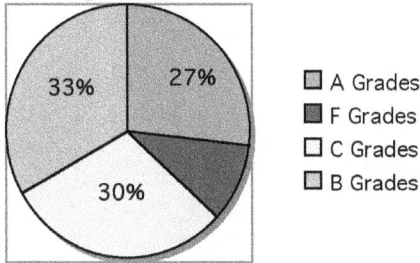

Line Chart

Average Test Score & Hours of Study

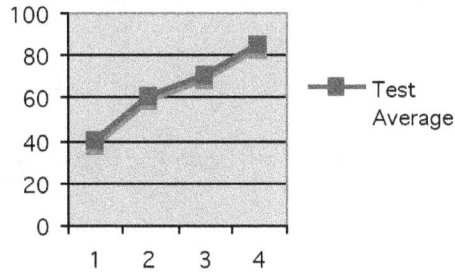

Line Chart (Time Series)

Average Salary and University Study

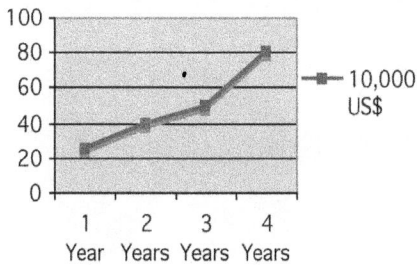

Column Chart

Profits by Region (in millions)

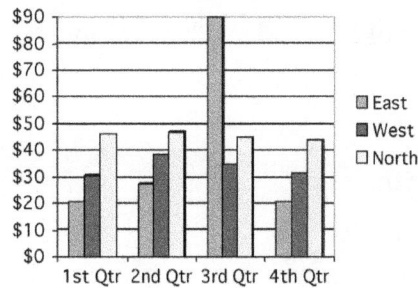

Bar Chart

Improvement by Division

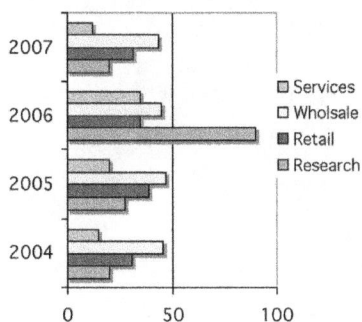

Area Chart

Performance by Region and Div.

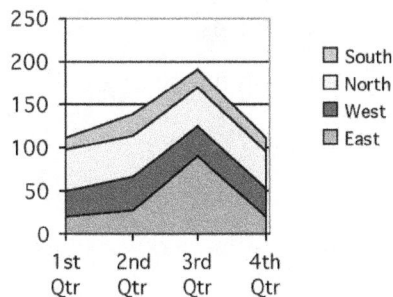

Economic Reasoning Questions 1.4

1. The three types of factual tools used by economists are:

a. _____

b. _____

c. _____

2. Which of these factual tools is demonstrated by each of the following examples?

a. The level of imports and exports between China and Japan

_____

b. Free trade agreements

_____

c. The effects of free trade with other countries

_____

d. Tariffs and quotas

_____

e. The effects of free trade on the UK plumbing industry

_____

3. Enter the missing terms.

a. A number that has an unknown or changeable value is called a(n)

_____.

b. A relationship between two variables in which their values increase and decrease together is referred to as a(n) _____ relationship.

c. A relationship between two variables in which the value of one decreases as the value of the other increases is called a(n) _____ relationship.

Theoretical Tools of Economics

The **theoretical tools** that economists use are economic *concepts* and economic *models*. An **economic concept** is a word or phrase that conveys an economic idea. The word is not always the same as the ordinary dictionary definition.

The most important of the theoretical tools for economists are economic models. Models may be in verbal, equation, or graphic form. An **economic model** is a simple way to show the cause-and-effect relationships of variables in a particular situation.

Models explaining relationships in a very simple way may be easier to understand but will carry less information and will be therefore less accurate. Models that contain more detail and are therefore more accurate may be however more difficult to understand. Verbal models, graphic or visual models, and equations are three different ways to express relationships between variables.

A *verbal model* is merely the expression of a relationship between variables using words. The relationship between height and weight in a population might be expressed merely in words. "On average in a given population as height increases weight will also increase." This will not always be true for individual examples of course; but in general the taller a person is the heavier they tend to be.

An *equation* is simply a statement, usually made with numbers and symbols. Any verbal model can be converted into an equation. For example, the area of a rectangle is its length multiplied by its width. This could also be expressed as the equation $A = L \times W$.

Albert Einstein's famous verbal model of relativity says that mass (m) is equivalent to energy (E), and the amount of energy contained in a piece of mass is equal to the mass multiplied with the square of the speed of light (c). This abstruse statement could be more simply expressed as the famous equation $E = mc^2$.

Visual or *graphic models* are created to convey information to the viewer by omitting information that is not important and focusing only on the information necessary for understanding. A map is one type of visual model of the real world. Some maps are very detailed, but perhaps more difficult to read. Other maps are quite simple to read, but may leave out details that one might like to know. Think of a map of your school. If a visitor only needed to find her way to the library from the entrance, only a very simple map showing the buildings and walkways would be necessary. More details are not necessary. The location of every tree, water fountain, and restroom will not help the visitor's understanding of the location of the library. However, if that visitor needed to use the restroom, a map without this detail would not be as useful.

Perhaps a more detailed map would be better? Imagine a huge map so detailed that it contained the location of every building, every tree, every rock, every desk, chair and table. Such a map would be very accurate and detailed in representing the real world, but what if it were as large as ten meters wide and weighed ten kilograms. Obviously, this extremely detailed map would be troublesome to use despite its accuracy and detail of the real world.

Other visual models work the same way; the less detailed the model, the easier it is to gain understanding. However, less detail means a possibly less accurate representation of the real world. On the other hand, more details might make a model a very accurate representation of reality, but we might want to avoid it becoming too complex to aid understanding.

Analytical diagrams are graphic models. An **economic diagram** is a graphic economic model showing how two or more variables relate to each other. The line graphs mentioned previously are commonly used graphic economic diagrams to show inverse or direct relationships between two economic variables.

Economic Reasoning Questions 1.5

1. Enter the missing terms.

a. An idea that has a particular meaning in economics that may be different from the common dictionary meaning is called an economic _____.

b. A simplified representation of the real world is referred to an as an economic

_____.

c. Economic models can be represented in three ways; _____,

_____ and _____.

2. Indicate whether the following examples are economic concepts or models.
Circle (M)odel or (C)oncept

a. M / C   Scarcity
b. M / C   Diagrams
c. M / C   Grades improve with study time
d. M / C   factor of production
e. M / C $V = L \times W \times H$ (volume of a rectangular space)

3. Indicate which type of representation (visual verbal or equation) the following economic models demonstrate.

a. More education leads to a higher salary.

_____

b. $M \times V = P \times Q$ (the quantity theory of money)

_____

c. A Supply and Demand Curve
   (the figure to the right)

_____

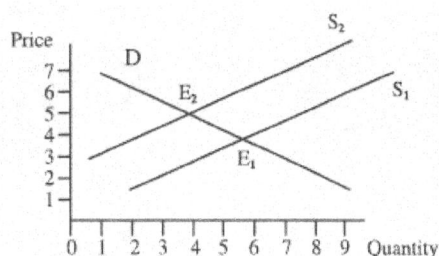

SECTION TWO

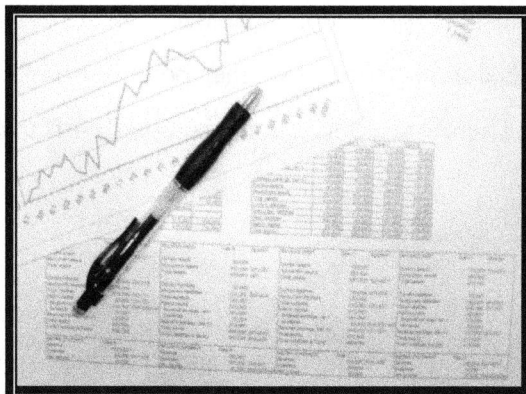

The Basic Economic Choices
Every Society Must Decide Upon

Economic Choices

As we described in the previous section, one way to define economics is the *science of choice*. We also reviewed the economic concept of **scarcity**, the condition that results from the fact that while our wants and needs are unlimited, the resources we need to produce the things we want and need are limited. Therefore some kind of economic system is necessary to choose how resources are used and which goods and services will be produced. The purpose of an economic system is to help make the difficult choices about how best to divide (or **allocate**) the resources available to that system and to make best use of those resources.

Allocation

The way in which a society *allocates* its scarce resources (according to the customs or personal tastes or preferences of its people) determines what that society produces. Choices are often difficult because in order to make a choice, any alternatives to that choice must be given up. The decision to devote resources to produce good X is also a decision sacrifice any other potential use for the resources required to produce good X. Therefore, every choice is a **trade-off** and has a cost.

Trade-Offs

Due to scarcity, the allocation choices a society makes involve *trade-offs*, which is a decision between one action and any possible alternatives to that action. Such decisions require us to consider all possible uses for a given quantity of a resource and choosing which would be the best or optimum use for the resource. If there were a societal demand for growing more corn, for example, the trade-off would be the sacrifice of land suitable for growing other vegetables or fruit.

As a result of resources being scarce, using resources to produce one thing means that other things will not be produced. Trade-offs don't only involve alternative uses for resources. A trade-off might occur in our lives if we have to decide on whether to study for a test or go out to a movie or a restaurant with our friends.

In many economies like those observed in Europe or the United States, consumers make most of the decisions about the allocation or distribution of resources. If for example people show a preference to eat more potatoes or corn then more land will be allocated for these products and the trade-off would be the loss of this land for other kinds of food.

Similarly, in a car-reliant society like the UK or the USA there is always a need for more roads and highways. This often means the loss of land that could be utilized for housing or recreational space. Moreover more cars result in more need for oil, more pollution in the air and therefore more pressure on medical services to combat the effects of pollution on the population. From this example alone we can see that all decisions carry costs, both direct and hidden, which will be explained in more detail further on.

In economic terms, the concept of trade-offs is expressed as **opportunity cost**.

Economic Reasoning Questions 2.1

1. We are forced to make trade-offs because of _____

2. If a society develops its military through government spending what are some of the trade-offs involved? _____

_____

_____

3. Give some examples of trade-offs you make with the precious resource of time.

_____

_____

_____

Opportunity Costs

An **opportunity cost** is the economic cost of a good or service produced measured by the value of the sacrificed alternative.

As an individual you make decisions every day about how to allocate a precious resource -- your time. If you decide to wake up and go to school you give up (or sacrifice) the *opportunity* to do something else. If you are at school you are not sleeping late, shopping, going to a movie or working a part-time job. All of these things would be considered an opportunity cost of going to school. Conversely, a decision to sleep late would have an opportunity cost of attending school.

Opportunity cost includes any sacrifices necessary to complete a given course of action. If for example you are studying to be a doctor or accountant, the opportunity cost is not only the money needed for college fees and the prices of textbooks but also the lost income from a salaried job or time spent on training with a sports team that you might be a member of. Your cost are not just financial, you will also lose the opportunity to spend time exercising   and   training   and spending 'quality time' with your friends on the team.

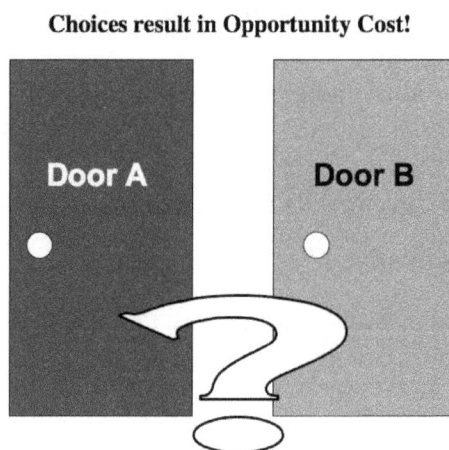

Choices result in Opportunity Cost!

In terms of money this quality time cannot be measured of course, but in terms of value to you this time may be very precious. Moreover, by studying you lose the opportunity to earn money and the chance to spend this money on music movies and the latest technological gadgets such as a new cell phone or the latest music player.

There is a famous expression, *"There is no such thing as a free lunch."* This refers to opportunity cost. You trade something for that lunch. This might be for example, the loss of your free time where you could be doing something else, the fact that you may have to listen to someone's sales pitch at lunch which could be extremely boring to you, or you may be asked to do something in return for someone else paying for your lunch, such as helping that person in a way that would take up even more of your time. In life everything that we do has an opportunity cost in terms of alternative choices. In short, because of scarcity, everything carries a cost and societies have to decide how best to serve its citizens.

Figure 2.2 - Scarcity requires allocation, which creates opportunity cost.

Connected Economic Concepts

Scarcity

⬇

Allocation (choices)

⬇

Opportunity Cost

The Production possibilities frontier (PPF)

Trade-offs and opportunity costs can be shown using an economic model called a production possibilities frontier. The **production possibility frontier** (or **PPF**) is the line on a graph showing the different **maximum** output combinations of goods or services that can be obtained from a fixed amount of resources. As with any model it is a simplified version of real world phenomena. For simplification purposes, a PPF assumes that an economy produces just two goods; and secondly, that technology and the quantity of resources are fixed.

Figure 2.2 - PPF

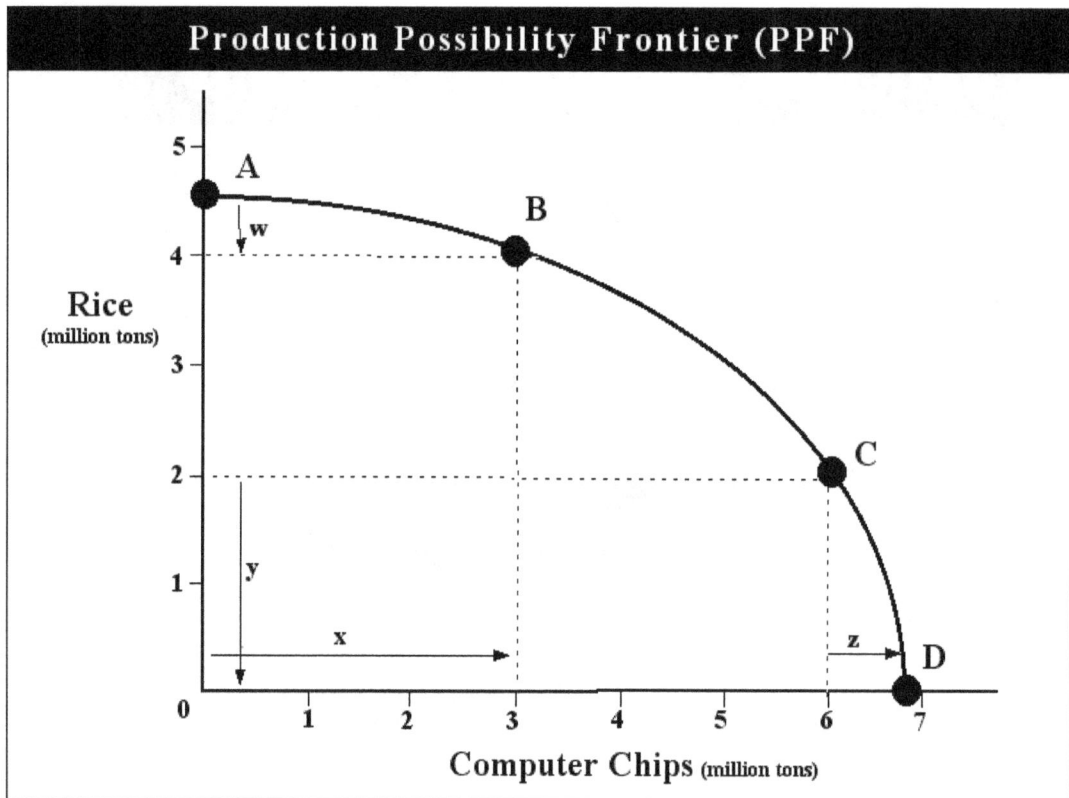

The graph shows the trade off between rice and the manufacture of computer chips and the losses incurred with shifting from one factor of production to another. Here we can compare the cost of producing one product against the resulting loss of not being able to produce another product. At point A there are about 4.5 million tons of rice produced and no resources allocated to computer chips.

At point B resources have been moved to the production of computer chips (land has been allocated to factory space, workers have been allocated for the factory etc.) and 3 million tons of computer chips (x) have been produced at a very small opportunity cost (w) of 0.5 tons of rice.

At point C resources for the production of computer chips are running out (no more land is available for the allocation of factory space, no more workers available). The opportunity costs of not producing rice have dramatically increased to 2 million tons of lost rice.

At point D, moving all resources into computer chip production at point D for less than one ton of computer chips has sacrificed all production of rice. This highlights the case of **increasing costs**.

Increasing Costs

With production comes increasing costs. An often difficult concept to understand in economics is that the more of a good that is produced, the *more* costly (in terms of opportunity cost) it is to produce more and more of that good.

Consider the following: more land is needed for the growing of food or factories, more workers are needed to work on the land or in the factories, more money is needed to pay the workers' wages or buy machinery for the farm or the factory and with limited resources this would of course lead to more cost in production. Moreover there would be the loss of alternative uses to this land (food production) or workers seen in terms of opportunity costs.

Resources don't transfer perfectly from the production of one good to another. An area of a country may be an area good for milk production but the same industry would be badly suited for an area that is climatically different.

Suppose this area is much warmer in summer then it would probably prove unsuitable for this industry. A re-allocation of this industry would result in problems such as some breeds of cows finding this climate difficult, and there might be added costs in extra refrigeration of the milk for example. Similarly fruit production in a warmer area of a country would be badly suited for an area of colder climate where the fruit would not grow as well resulting in lower annual production figures.

Economic Reasoning Questions 2.2

1. What are the possible opportunity costs involved with the following:
   (Hint: think of possible alternative uses for the resources required for each action)

ex. Constructing a new classroom building
   _____*Constructing a new gymnasium*_____

a. Baking a chocolate cake

_____

b. Buying a new DVD in a shop

_____

c. Planting herbs in a garden or on a balcony in a city apartment

_____

d. Studying hard for an economics test

_____

e. Attending an economics class

_____

f. Paying taxes

_____

2. Trade offs, opportunity costs and growth.

The country of Ruritania has the following choices in production.

	Music player	Cell phone
A	0	180
B	20	170
C	40	155
D	60	135
E	80	100
F	100	60
G	120	0

Use this chart to plot each of these points and draw the economy's production possibility frontier. Label each point A, B, C, etc on your chart.

Label the horizontal axis music players scale this from 0 to 120 in 10 unit increments. Scale the vertical axis for Cell phones 0 to 180 in 30 unit increments

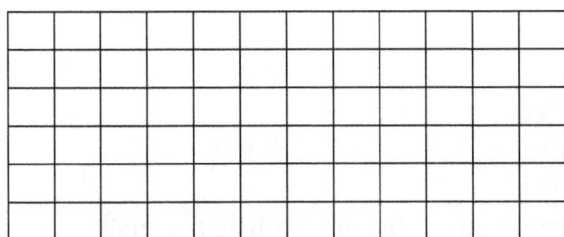

a. Starting at point A on your graph, what is the opportunity cost of 20 music players? _____

b. Starting at point B on your graph, what is the opportunity cost of 20 music players?

_____

c. Starting at point C on your graph, what is the opportunity cost of 20 music players?

_____

d. Starting at point D on your graph, what is the opportunity cost of 20 music players?

_____

e. The trade-off between music players and cell phones is an example of _____ opportunity costs.

The country of Hobbitron has the following choices in production.

	Music player	Cell phone
A	0	180
B	20	150
C	40	120
D	60	90
E	80	60
F	100	30
G	120	0

Use this chart to plot each of these points and draw the economy's production possibility frontier. Label each point A, B, C, etc on your chart.

Label the horizontal axis music players scale this from 0 to 120 in 10 unit increments. Scale the vertical axis for Cell phones 0 to 180 in 30 unit increments

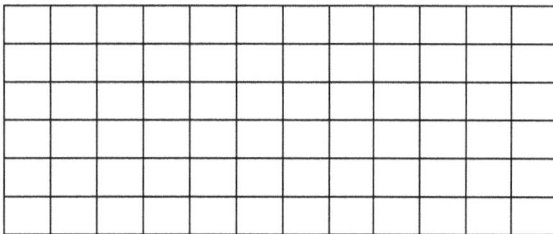

a. Starting at point A on your graph, what is the opportunity cost of 20 music players?

_____

b. Starting at point B on your graph, what is the opportunity cost of 20 music players?

_____

c. Starting at point C on your graph, what is the opportunity cost of 20 music players?

_____

d. Starting at point D on your graph, what is the opportunity cost of 20 music players?

_____

e. The trade-off between music players and cell phones is an example of

_____ opportunity costs.

The Basic Economic Questions

Considering these points, society has to make very careful and specific decisions about the best use of its precious and limited resources. In the allocation of resources there are three basic economic questions that must be successfully answered:

W**hat** to produce? **How** to produce? And **for whom** to produce?

What to Produce?

Precisely what goods and services to produce (and therefore what not to produce) and in what amounts is the first question that any economic system. Different societies have different wants and needs that are often culturally dependent. What to produce is the question concerning the decisions made by a society about what particular goods and services to produce given its limited resources.

So who answers this question? There are multiple possibilities. A government leader or committee might supply an answer to this question; the answer may be based on custom or tradition, or perhaps by the interactions between buyers and sellers. However, any functional economic system must provide an answer to this question.

How to Produce?

After a society has determined what goods and services to produce, it must then decide precisely how to best produce the products demanded by that society. *How to produce* is the question relating to the methods used by an economy about what (and how much of) particular goods and services are produced with its limited resources.

A very important factor in answering this question is a society's endowments of labor and capital. In technologically advanced countries, workers have a relatively larger share of capital (equipment, software, technology) at their disposal. A nation such as this is described as a **capital-intensive economy**. Access to capital tends to make workers in capital-intensive economies more productive, and therefore labor tends to be more expensive.

Conversely, a country that has a lesser stock of capital but has relatively large number of people willing to work (or *labor pool*) is described as a **labor-intensive economy**. A large labor pool with less access to capital results in less expensive labor costs.

A nation will use labor-intensive techniques if it has a lot of unemployed or underemployed labor, for example non-industrialized countries in less developed countries such as Bangladesh or Sudan. Whereas many industrialized countries in the North like the U.K. or the U.S. will use capital-intensive production techniques. Consider the following example:

Answering the "what" question, two cities in different parts of the world recently made a decision to produce the same product: a new subway line. In Kyoto, Japan (a capital intensive country), the answer to the "how" question was to use giant tunneling machines to dig the new subway line. However, in Calcutta, India (a relatively labor intensive-country) the answer to the "how" question was to use hundreds of human laborers digging their subway tunnel with picks and shovels.

The example above illustrates how even an identical product might be produced differently depending on what resources are available to a society. Very often a country's labor and capital resources will be a determinant in which products that country has a *comparative advantage* in producing.

A country can help increase its amount of capital (or *capital stock*) by encouraging savings (in banks, stocks, bonds, etc.). If people save they place their money in banks and they earn **interest** (usually as a percentage of the money they invested). The money put into banks by individuals (and also businesses) is then available to businesses (or *firms*) that can borrow money to invest in capital equipment.

Governments or local communities can invest in **infrastructure** to make an economy more productive. China, for example has successfully invested money into future development by encouraging growth in its infrastructure.

Infrastructure

Infrastructure can be seen as an economy's store of capital. Much of this is publicly owned and provides services to companies and private consumers. Infrastructure includes communications systems, highways, electric power, water supplies, educational institutions, and health services.

A country's wealth can be easily observed by the condition of its infrastructure compare Afghanistan to Australia for example. How we produce also depends on the technology that is available to a society. For example, improved technology allows an economy to produce more. Witness the recent rise in production of countries such as China and India, countries with an abundant supply of the precious resource of labor.

Societies must constantly make decisions on whether to concentrate on producing short-term consumer goods or more long term capital goods. Balancing these two concerns determines whether a society is able to grow efficiently. The **production possibilities frontier** can also be used to show the trade-off between consumer and capital goods.

For Whom to Produce?

This is the question of how a society determines who gets how much of the goods and services produced by that society. Many nations are faced with the problem of whether to allocate spending to their military to increase their security or to allocate their scarce resources to education or health services. It is difficult to balance spending between creating a strong secure nation and matching societal needs in terms of hospitals and schools for example.

Clearly there is a dilemma here. Society must examine its needs, decide what goods to produce to meet these needs and in so doing examine whether the goods produced are 'useful' for society. The different ways that an economy chooses to spend money determines which groups in the economy benefit – the military, the poor, the rich, the old or the sick for example.

Economic Goals for Society

Just as individual citizens have goals for their lives – achieving a good education, finding a good job, raising a family, living in a pleasant area of town, so society has economic goals. Included in these goals are growth, efficiency and achieving full employment of labor. There are also goals known as socioeconomic goals involving concepts such as equity, which is sometimes defined as justice or fairness.

Growth

For any society economic growth is important. Economic growth is important in that it helps an economy to produce more goods and services and in the same way helps the people in an economy to buy or consume more goods. Economic growth is an increase in the production capacity of the economy.

One way to increase economic growth is to slow down or defer current spending by individuals for consumer goods and allocate more resources into producing capital goods such as highways or airports.

One way to demonstrate this visually would be to use a PPF diagram like the one in figure 2.2a below. Point A (or any other point on the curved line) indicates maximum efficiency and output. B indicates a point of unattainable output, as it is greater than the maximum. However if economic growth enabled a greater number of productive resources to become available then *all* points on the PPF would increase, resulting in a new curve further to the right, as demonstrated in figure 2.2b below.

Figure 2.2a   **Figure 2.2b**

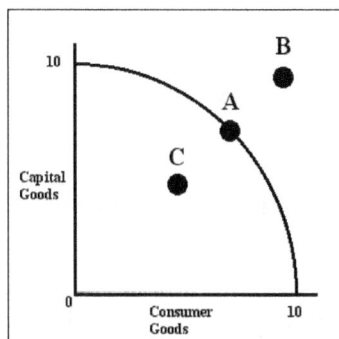   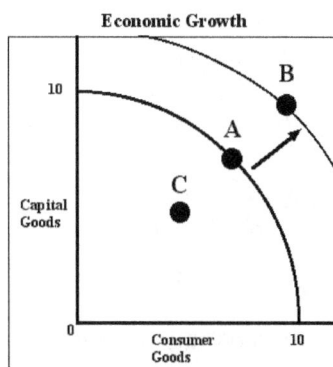

Efficiency

To use all resources efficiently in a society is also one of society's goals. The efficient allocation of resources is important for maximum economic growth. Efficiency is getting the most out of all available resources or maximizing the output.

As a model to illustrate this, any point inside the production possibilities frontier (such as point C) represents inefficiency. If a society is not using all its available resources then it is seen to be inefficient. Not utilizing all available labor is a sign of inefficiency, so full employment is another of society's goals.

Full Employment

Full employment is the employment of nearly everyone who is willing to work. Achieving full employment will help an economy to attain full output and economic growth. An unemployment level of not more than 5-6% is considered full employment.

Historically, high unemployment rates have led to such societal problems as poverty and violence. For example after the Wall Street Crash of 1929 the US suffered high levels of unemployment during the Great Depression. It was estimated that around 25% of the working population were unemployed in 1932.

This had a devastating effect on the economy and also on the American citizenry. Clearly effective measures were needed and this led to landmark laws known as the New Deal being passed by President Franklin Roosevelt and Congress.

These new laws helped start massive job and housing programs and focused on the protection of the sick and the unemployed. Social Security gave help to poor and elderly American citizens and Unemployment Insurance helped alleviate temporary loss of work as well as helping unemployed citizens continue to purchase goods and services.

If unemployment exists, an economy is not effectively utilizing its given resources. To show this as an illustrative economic model this can be seen as producing at a point inside its production possibilities frontier (such as point C on the diagrams above).

Price Stability

Unstable prices can prevent an economy from achieving its maximum production possibilities, witness the terrible conditions in Germany in the 1920s after the First World War. Price stability is a constant average level of prices for all goods and services.

The continuing rise in prices for goods and services is known as inflation, which results in a reduction in the purchasing power of money. Inflation lowers the standard of living unless wages are increased in line with inflation.

Socioeconomic Goals

A socioeconomic goal is a type of social goal that has important economic dimensions. It is up to each society to decide which socioeconomic goals are important enough to pursue. The influential economist John Maynard Keynes (1883-1946) advocated that some government intervention is desirable in fighting the worst economic inequities.

Some examples of socioeconomic goals are:

Environmental protection, which insures the quality of the natural environment with standards for clean and safe air, water, and food and also preventing and reducing pollution management of hazardous waste.

Economic security / financial planning policies require households to save portions of their income for later uses such as medical expenses or post-retirement income (pensions).

Economic equity - ideals and values applied in economic circumstances influenced by principles of ethics and fairness.

Economic justice - policies designed to prevent exploitation of workers human rights, particularly those of women and children.

Economic freedom - The ability to pursue one's economic self-interest without interference or regulation from government or other authority.

The creation of economic IGO's such as the World Bank were inspired by Keynesian economic ideals. Other international institutions like UNICEF and UNESCO (as well as the efforts of countless NGOs) are increasingly focusing on socioeconomic issues such as long-term environmental protection and poverty relief.

Economic Reasoning Questions 2.3

1. These problems need solving by one of the basic economic questions:

a. A government has a surplus in its budget

The _____ question.

b. A leading car company is thinking of updating some its old computer systems in its automobile factories

The _____ question.

c. A fast food company wants to replace its old fat fryers

The _____ question.

d. Low fat food is becoming more popular with consumers

The _____ question.

2. What are the four primary economic goals of economics?

a._____   b. _____

c._____   d. _____

3. Indicate which goals the following statements reflects:

a. The Nikkei index reports a 3% increase in stock prices   _____

b. Inflation needs to be brought down in the UK   _____

c. New computer systems are introduced into all government offices   _____

d. In parts of Holland workers losing jobs due to 'downsizing' are to be targeted in a new government program to find them jobs   _____

4. Why is reducing unemployment an economic goal?

_____

_____

5. Reducing unemployment leads to the economic goal of

6. The production possibility frontier below shows the trade-offs involved in the production of beans and eggs.

a. Indicate points that correspond to the following:

Unemployment (point A)

Full employment (point B)

An Unattainable level of output (point C)

Beans

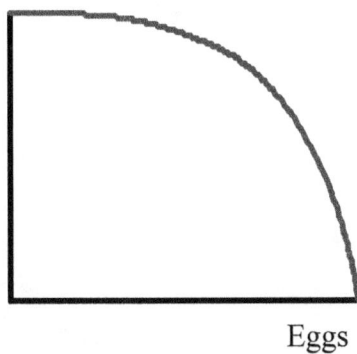

Eggs

7. The PPF frontier below shows an economy's trade-off between cars and trucks.

Cars

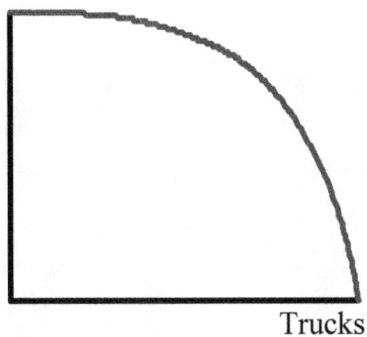

Trucks

a. Label a point A that corresponds to efficient production.

Label a point B that corresponds to inefficient production.

8. Place a check to indicate examples of efficient production?

a. _____A company producing goods at the lowest possible cost

b. _____A two-hour break for lunch

c. _____An unemployment rate of 13%

d. _____Fully using all available resources

9. Give examples of productive investments that may be carried out by the following:

a. A university

i. _____

ii. _____

b. The government

i. _____

ii. _____

c. A local government

i. _____

ii. _____

d. A carmaker .

i. _____

ii. _____

e. A law office

i. _____

ii. _____

SECTION 3

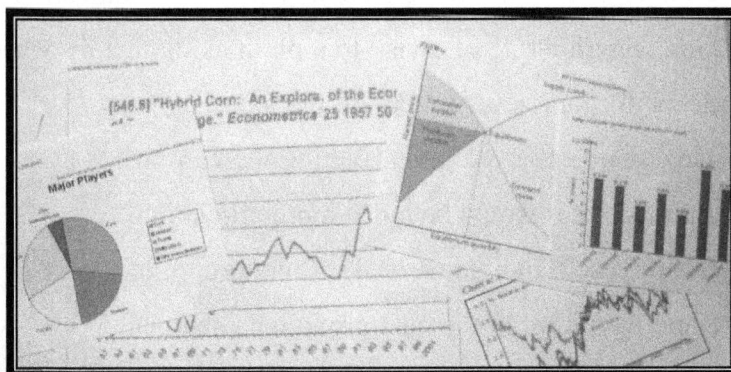

Systems for Answering the Basic Economic Questions

Why Are Economic Systems Necessary?

A simple answer to this question would be that economic systems are necessary to organize and coordinate a society's economic choices and activities.

In the past skilled workers like the Chippendale family in England would build furniture themselves or the Martin family in the USA would make guitars or the Wedgwood family would make pottery. All these activities would take place in self-contained workshops. A product would be started, finished and sold from that workshop in a self-contained production process.

The **Industrial Revolution** introduced factory systems with machinery and technology making production faster. Factory systems evolved, cities grew larger around the factories, workers moved to the cities to find work, leaving gaps in agriculture production leading to cheaper agricultural products being imported from other countries and factory goods in turn being exported creating trade systems.

Adam Smith, the father of classical trade theory, wrote of specialization in 1776 in *The Wealth of Nations.* Smith wrote of a visit to a pin-making factory where each individual worker was performing every step of the pin-making process (cutting the wire, sharpening the point, putting the cap on, etc.). Smith pointed out that that it would be much more efficient to divide up the workers by each individual tasks (one group of workers only cut wire and pass it on to the next group who sharpen the points and pass them on the next group, an so on). By doing so, the workers of the pin-making factory were able to produce far more pins in much less time than when they were working individually.

As industrialized systems progressed in the 20th century more innovations in production emerged, such as Henry Ford's famous assembly line for producing automobiles. This has led to workers being involved in just one stage of the final production process. This is often referred to as *specialization*.

Specialization

In the search for greater efficiency in production we have become more dependent on others to support and assist us. In the production of most products, there is a division of labor into specialized tasks.

Specialization results in greater efficiency and lower production costs. Specialization also can apply to nations producing those goods and services that their resources are best suited to produce, in the case of Japan this can be automobiles, video games, or TVs and DVD players. As purported by Adam Smith and Henry

Ford, specialization leads to increased production and in order to take advantage of it, economic societies need to decide who should specialize in doing what.

This comes from the basic belief of the market that if two people (or two countries) produce goods that they are most adept at producing, they will do better in these production areas as they are more efficient at producing these products relative to the other. They can then exchange these goods keeping their costs low and so enable their business or economy to grow. The demand for their products will therefore grow as they remain competitive in the area that they are best suited to produce goods in.

Countries import goods because these goods are either not available at home or are too expensive to produce competitively. They also import goods that may be on offer at home but have different design features, for example European furniture stores offer goods in the U.S. which are arguably similar to those on offer in U.S. home improvement centers, but the style of these goods are attractive to many us consumers.

Similarly, businesses and farms in less developed countries are sometimes able to offer cheaper products and services than those produced in the U.S. although the U.S. could produce the same products. The U.S. may decide that because these products are produced more cheaply in other countries the U.S. should produce more expensive or sophisticated items of food.

Developed countries usually find it economically viable to therefore import semi-finished goods or products that can be assembled into finished products. The reasoning here is that these semi-finished goods and services can be initially produced more cheaply by developing countries. Wages for workers in less developed countries are comparatively less than those in the North as workers tend to be lower skilled.

As wages and skills tend to be higher in the North it makes sense for certain products to be imported from countries that can produce these products more cheaply. The North can thus specialize in concentrating on products that are more sophisticated and can be sold more expensively.

As we have seen production costs are affected by land labor and capital. Developing countries are able to offer cheaper labor and resources that are far more expensive in industrialized countries. Relatively speaking industrialized countries because of their longer history of development are able to offer production techniques and capital that cannot be achieved in developing countries.

Countries therefore specialize in what that country produces best, and enter into trade with other countries exchanging goods and services.

Can There Be Too Much Specialization?

Increasing and excessive specialization can begin to have negative effects as well. In Section Two we explored the economic concept of *increasing costs* of specialization, but there are other potential costs of excessive specialization as well. Too much specialization of labor can have a major negative effect: *boredom!* Imagine if your job all day every day was to tighten one little screw on a machine part on an assembly line. Often good factory managers will have their assembly line workers specialize in several different tasks that they can switch and rotate the boring jobs between several workers.

Depending on your philosophy, you might believe that too much specialization could make you depend too much on others for the things you need. Historically speaking, not too long ago most people (or at least most villages) grew their own food, made their own clothes, and built their own homes. How many of these activities have you done today? Some people believe that economic interdependence is a good thing that will make society more cooperative; others believe that too much dependence on others to provide for your needs is risky or perhaps even counter to human nature.

Science fiction author Robert Heinlein expressed this sentiment in his 1973 book *Time Enough for Love:*

> A human being should be able to change a diaper, … design a building, … balance accounts, build a wall, set a bone, comfort the dying, take orders, give orders, cooperate, act alone, solve equations, analyze a new problem, … program a computer, cook a tasty meal, fight efficiently, die gallantly. Specialization is for insects.

Of course, the character saying this was supposed to be over a thousand years old!

The Concepts of Absolute and Comparative Advantage

Absolute Advantage

Another concept Adam Smith introduced to is the concept of **absolute advantage,** which is one indicator of exactly what a person or region or country should specialize in producing. A producer is said to have an absolute advantage relative to another producer if they can produce more of a good or service than the other with the *same* amount of resources. For example, two people were each given identical stacks of fifty sheets of paper and you told then to make as many paper airplanes as they could in the next five minutes. Person A manages to fold all fifty sheets of paper into fifty paper airplanes in five minutes. Person B however has only managed to make thirty paper airplanes in the same amount of time. We can say from this example that Person A has an absolute advantage over Person B in paper airplane-making, because Person A can produce more than Person B given the same amount of resources (in this case their labor, paper and time allotted).

The U.S. is a good example of a country having absolute advantage in the production of many products due to its status as an economic superpower. In theory, if it so desired, the U.S. could produce almost any product faster than many other countries given its resources of land, labor, and capital. However, it is clear that the U.S. has chosen to not specialize producing some goods and services, even though it may have an absolute advantage in doing so. For example, currently consumers in the U.S. have a great demand for TVs, yet very few are produced inside the U.S. Why?

Couldn't the U.S. produce more TVs than Mexico or China if it wanted to? Yes, the U.S. probably *could* produce more TVs than Mexico or maybe even China, but *at what cost?* What kinds of things would Americans have to give up producing; or as we have previously discussed in Section Two, what would be the **opportunity cost** of attempting to out-produce China in TVs? Probably the opportunity cost to the U.S. would be high to pursue such production. This suggests that absolute advantage is perhaps not the best indicator of what people or nations should specialize in.

Comparative Advantage

The concept of comparative advantage is most often attributed to the economist David Ricardo who wrote *Principles of Political Economy and Taxation* in 1817. Ricardo theorized that even if a country could produce everything more efficiently than another country (i.e. had absolute advantage), it would still benefit from specializing in what it was best at producing (in terms of costs) and trading with other nations.

Turning back to opportunity costs, we have seen that we have choices in what to devote our time and resources to, and this results in the loss of other choices that we may or may not have pursued. The loss of these choices is known as opportunity costs. So it is with businesses and nations. A nation given its labor, capital or land could chose to produce or manufacture a variety of goods or services. However this leads to the sacrifice of other products that cannot be produced. The UK if it chooses in a given working hour could produce 2000 liters of beer or 1000 liters of milk. If it chose to produce 2000 liters of beer then the opportunity cost is 1000 liters of milk. The UK then has a comparative advantage in producing beer as it can produce twice as much beer than milk in a given hour. Conversely if it produced 1000 liters of milk the opportunity cost would be 2000 liters of beer. Clearly it makes economic sense for the UK to produce beer.

A producer has a **comparative advantage** relative to another producer if he or she can produce a good or service at a lower opportunity cost than the other. The U.S.

may have an absolute advantage in producing toys and textiles but China's opportunity costs are lower, China's factories operate on far cheaper running costs than American factories and China's factory workers earn lower wages than American factory workers so China therefore has a **comparative advantage** – China produces many of the same items that the U.S. can, but can do so more cheaply. Individuals, regions, and nations tend to specialize in the production of those things in which they have a comparative advantage - witness the emerging economies of China and India.

Economic Reasoning Questions 3.1

1. Indicate which of the following is true of Absolute and Comparative Advantage.

a. Someone who can produce a good or a service at a lower relative cost is said to have a (an) _____ in the production of that good or service.

b. Someone who can produce two kinds of products more efficiently than another producer has a (an)_____ advantage in the production of both goods.

2. If China can produce toys and machinery more efficiently than South Africa then South Africa should specialize in a product that it has the greatest _____ advantage.

3. A leather bag company states that they offer the best products in term of price and efficiency at meeting customer orders. An economist would say that they _____ in the production of that good and that leads to greater _____ and _____ costs in producing it.

4. Tony is the best plumber and tire fitter in town. He can fit tires or install a new shower in 2 hours. George is a good tire fitter and plumber but nowhere near as good as Tony, he takes 3 hours to fit tires and 4 hours to install a shower.   Tony charges $70 an hour for his plumbing rate and George charges $40 hour for fitting tires.

a. In terms of lost income from installing showers, how much would it cost Tony to fit his own tires? _____

b. How much would Tony have to pay George to fit his own tires? _____

c. Who should fit Tony's tires? Why? _____

d. In terms of lost income from fitting tires, how much would it cost George to install his own shower? _____

e. How much would George have to pay Tony to install George's shower? _____

f. Who should install George's shower? Why? _____

g. Does either George or Tony have an absolute advantage? _____

h. What does each have a comparative advantage in doing?

Tony_____   George _____

i. What activities should each specialize in?

Tony _____   George _____

Interdependence

Every person (or economy) has a comparative advantage at some activity. A mother may be able to clean the family car better than her young son but she is no doubt a busy person and so in order to lower her workload she may be willing to pay him money to clean the car. She is dependent on him in ways such as these just as he is dependent on her for her knowledge of hygiene, nutrition and well-being.

As children need their mothers for certain things and mothers may need children for certain things so we become dependent on one another – we exchange the skills we are best at. Specialization tends to encourage businesses and countries to trade and exchange goods and services that they are best suited to produce for goods they are not best suited to produce resulting in a mutually rewarding trading system

In other words *specialization* results in **interdependence**, which is the relationship between individuals and institutions in a country or between countries that arises because of specialization of production.

As a result of the myriad of skills generated by society and nations and the reliance each has on others for trade and commerce we can see that interdependence requires an economic system to coordinate everyone's activities.

> **Connected Economic Concepts**
>
> **Scarcity**
> ↓
> **Allocation (choices)**
> ↓
> **Opportunity Cost**
> ↓
> **Comparative Advantage**
> ↓
> **Specialization**
> ↓
> **Interdependence**

This is a very difficult problem to resolve as for example any successful football manager or business entrepreneur knows and so leads to what is known as the *coordination problem*.

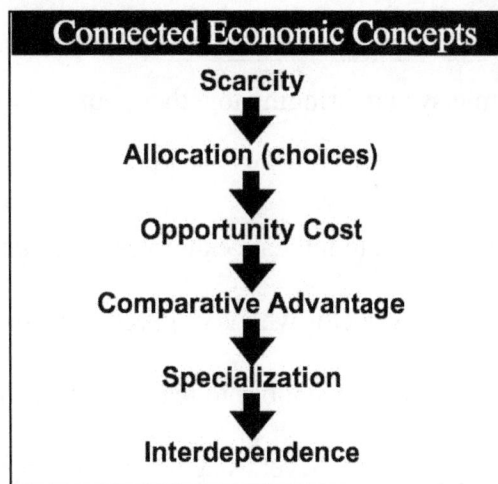

The Coordination Problem

This is the managing of various groups of production in order to form a functioning unit where all the specialized activities of people interact seamlessly. Tomato producers need buyers for their tomatoes, buyers need to package the tomatoes in cans, canning companies need suppliers to provide cans, and so the process continues. A slowdown in one area leads to problems elsewhere. By solving this problem with effective coordination an economic system is able to answer the basic economic questions.

Economic Reasoning Questions 3.2

1. If one person does one part of the production then they will need others to help in another part of the production. That person is _____ on other people to finish the job.

2. As the degree of _____increases in society, we become more and more_____.

3. The _____ problem refers to the challenge faced by an economic system bringing together people's specialized activities so that everyone's wants and needs are met.

4. Place a check to indicate examples of the *coordination problem*

a. _____ A doctor who is required to be on-call to the hospital for a 12-hour shift.

b. _____ People choose to leave the labor force to take care of children full-time.

c. _____ Truck drivers stage a month-long strike.

d. _____ A bakery breaks its contract to supply a restaurant's bread.

e. _____ A university professor decides to take early retirement and stop teaching.

f. _____ Severe weather damages a country's rail links preventing the movement of people and cargo.

What Are the Principal Types of Economic Systems?

Specialization and *interdependence* need system coordination to solve the coordination problem and form a functioning economic system. Globalization has brought this into sharp focus. Countries do not function in a vacuum; they need support from other countries and sign agreements for trade or security. As economies have evolved, three basic types of economic systems have been identified. These are known as **market economies**, **centrally directed economies** and **traditional economies**.

Market Economy

A market economy is an economic system in which the basic questions of *what, how*, and *for whom* to produce are answered mainly by buyers and sellers interacting in markets.

Market economies are often called *capitalist* or *free enterprise* economies. The nations within the European Community can be identified primarily as market economies, as can the United States. There are three requirements for a market economy to function.

The first of these requirements is the ability for individuals to own property, usually referred to as a system of **private property**, which is the exclusive right of someone to use a scarce resource or good in whatever manner they think best, provided that they follow the law of the land.

Secondly, in a market system, ownership of property must be *transferable*, or in other words, it can be freely traded or sold to others.

Thirdly, individuals in a market system are allowed to pursue their economic *self-interest*, to act on their desire to receive the most satisfaction for their economic interactions (often determined by a desire for the greatest **profits**).

A Centrally Directed Economy

This type of economy (also referred to as a *command economy*) is an economic system in which the basic questions of what, how, and for whom to produce are answered primarily by governmental authority.   In a centrally directed economy, some kind of government *planning committee* or *agency* usually decides how to allocate the society's resources. The government decides the quantity and what types of products to produce and also sets prices.

While this description might be applied to many historical societies under an absolute ruler, we tend to think of examples of economies like these as resembling the former Soviet Union during most of the 20th century. Central planning was required to answer the basic economic questions because the Marxist-Leninist doctrine on which this society was based called for an end to most private property and limitations to an individual's ability to pursue economic self-interest. These so-called *communist* systems included the Chinese economy under Mao Zedong in the mid 20th century, Vietnam for much of the late 20th century, and the economies of North Korea and Cuba today. The hope of the founders of these economic systems was that economic self-interest could be replaced by a desire to act in the best interests of society. Unfortunately, many of these economies were never able to deliver the level of standard of living that their societies wanted. The early 21st century has thus seen many of these former centrally planned economies attempting to make the transition towards more market-based systems.

A Traditional Economy

Tradition is very strong in many less developed countries trying to industrialize. In many of these countries the basic questions of *what*, *how*, and *for whom* to produce are answered not by market interactions or government agencies but by custom and tradition.

Consider a country like India, which for centuries divided labor resources through a caste system. The types of jobs that were available to people depended on the social class into which their family belonged to. Today, India's constitution guarantees equality of opportunity for all citizens but traditional practices are often deeply ingrained in a society, particularly one struggling with the pressures of poverty and overpopulation.

Religious belief can also be influential to an economic system both indirectly and directly. The Islamic code of law Shari'a has been incorporated into the civil law of many countries that governs their economic systems. Countries such as Saudi Arabia, Iran and Malaysia have adopted elements of Shari'a into their business law. *Islamic banking,* for example, allows the flow of financial capital from depositors to borrowers for investment, while abiding by Islamic principles such as the prohibition on charging interest on loans.

Mixed Economies

In reality, very few economic systems are exclusively market, centrally planned, or traditional. Most economies are in fact a mixture of market, centrally directed, and traditional elements. A **mixed economy** is identified as an economic system where questions of *what, how,* and *for whom* to produce are mainly answered by a mixture of market forces with governmental direction and/or custom and tradition.

Economies like the U.S., Europe, and Japan are primarily market systems but of course there is some government involvement in the production of public goods and services (e.g. parks, education, mass transit). Tradition also has an influence on the types of labor people in market systems tend to specialize in. For example, in the U.S. nursing has traditionally been viewed as a career choice for women and dentistry for men. While these trends are changing, the point is that gender really does not really determine who would be a better nurse or a dentist, but traditional views of gender roles can still be influential, even in a predominantly market economy.

One type of mixed economy is referred to as **socialism** - an economic system allowing private ownership and free enterprise alongside extensive government ownership and involvement in key sectors of the economy. There are varying degrees of socialism (as measured by the extent of government ownership and involvement in the economy).

Another example of mixed economies is countries in transition from centrally planned to more market based economies. Nations such as China, and Vietnam are becoming more identifiable as mixed economies.

Economic Reasoning Questions 3.3

1. Indicate whether the following are examples of how market (M), centrally directed (C) or traditional (T) economies answer the three basic economic questions

a. _____Sumo wrestlers in Japan are men.

b. _____Before a Pharaoh died in Egypt they used to order a pyramid to be built for a final resting place.

c. _____A son takes over his father's business when the father retires from work.

d. _____A new movie is shown in town.

e. _____The city you live in builds a new park.

f. _____Sony develops a new game.

2. Think of a common good or service that is produced in your country. (beef, rice, movies, etc.) and then think of three ways in which the government influences the production and sale of that product.

Product: _____

Government influence:

a. _____

b. _____

c. _____

How Does a Market System Answer the Three Basic Economic Questions?

A market economy determines the three basic economic questions (*what, how &
for whom*) when output is allocated based on the interaction between producers and
consumers in the marketplace. Most would agree that a market economy should have
a limited amount of government interference.   Just how much government
interference is desirable however, is the subject of much debate.

A **marketplace** (**market**) can be seen as a network of dealings between buyers
and sellers of a resource or product (good or service). These interactions may take
place at a particular location such as a certain street in a town or a shopping mall; or
this interaction could take place through communication at a distance with no face-to-
face contact between buyers and sellers such as Internet commerce or international
currency and stock exchanges.

How do Markets Function in the First Place?

The core concept that drives a market economy to function is the concept of
incentives. An **incentive** is a motivation to attempt an action or to refrain from
attempting an action. There are many kinds of incentives. There are moral incentives
which are based on what one believes is right or wrong, social incentives which are
based on how you want others to perceive you, and of course, financial incentives
which are based on financial gain or loss. Incentives are the driving force behind
human behavior and rational humans will normally respond to incentives if they
believe it is in their benefit to do so. In a market economy the primary incentive that
allows a market system to function is the *profit incentive*.

Profits provide the incentive for producers to produce goods and services. If a
company can make more money from selling goods than it costs them to produce
those goods, then that company is making a profit from their production. Thus, price
is the most important components of the profit incentive. A rise in price is generally
an incentive to produce more and a drop in price to produce less. In a market

economy prices and the profit incentive determine how scarce resources are allocated to the production of different goods and services.

The Product Market and the Factor Market

A market economy is actually two markets working in tandem. These two markets are identified as **product markets** and **factor markets.** These two markets demonstrate how businesses and consumers interact and depend on each other to make a market system function.

The Product Market

A **product market** is something we are all familiar with as consumers because it is in this market where we purchase our everyday goods and services from businesses. In product markets businesses (or *firms*) are the sellers and consumers (or *households*) are the buyers. This is the market in which finished (or final) goods and services are exchanged between businesses and households in return for payment. This is the market where consumers purchase the goods that they desire, and in which businesses attempt to produce products that consumers will want to buy.

A **household** is an economic unit consisting of an individual or a family. This unit is both self-contained and reliant on other forces for its survival. The way in which households interact with businesses is another good example of interdependence; both need one another.

The Factor Market

In **factor markets** businesses are mainly buyers and mainly households are sellers. It is in this market in which businesses obtain all of the resources necessary to produce their goods and services that they intend to sell. Some of the sales in factor markets are business to business sales of capital equipment or other semi-finished components necessary for production of the finished product; but households/consumers are the owners of most of the resources purchased by businesses.

This might seem confusing at first, as a consumer what resources do you own or control that you might consider selling to a business? In order for consumers to purchase the things that they want and need, they will need income. Households have several choices on how to raise the income they need. Money paid by businesses to households is referred to as *factor payments*.

The one resource that nearly all households have to sell is their **labor**. Any sort of job or employment in return for payment is the sale of one's labor services to a business. The factor payment for labor services is referred to as *salary or wages*.

Perhaps you or your family owns a piece of **land** (or *real estate*) such as farmland, a vacant lot, or a building of some type. In exchange for payment, you could allow someone to make use of that land (outside of your household), such as raising crops on the farmland, living in an apartment, or running a business in the building you own. The factor payment for land use is referred to as *rent.*

Do you have any money saved in a bank account (or perhaps invested in stocks and bonds)? If so you are making your money available for businesses to borrow to pay for things such as start-up costs or investing in new software or equipment (also known as **capital)**. Your saving (or investing) could also be described as providing capital services to businesses, and the factor payment for such services is referred to as *interest*.

The **factor market** is a market in which land, labor, and capital resources as well as semi-finished products are bought and sold. In this market producers seek to acquire the necessary resources to assemble their finished product. Whether it is a site for a factory (requiring land) or some natural resource (oil, steel, or soybeans, for example) or the human resources (manual labor, salesmen, managers), these are all examples of resources that are sold in the factor markets.

The Circular Flow of the Economy

As a good example of interdependence we see that in a market economy businesses/firms and consumers/households both buy from and sell to each other. Households provide the resources that businesses need, land, labor and capital; and businesses provide the goods and services that households need such as food, clothing, entertainment and transportation for example. In this way markets are **circular**.

The basic functioning of a market economy can be shown as a **circular flow diagram.** This is an analytical diagram (model) showing the economic relationships between the major sectors of an economic system.

Figure 4.1 The Circular Flow Diagram

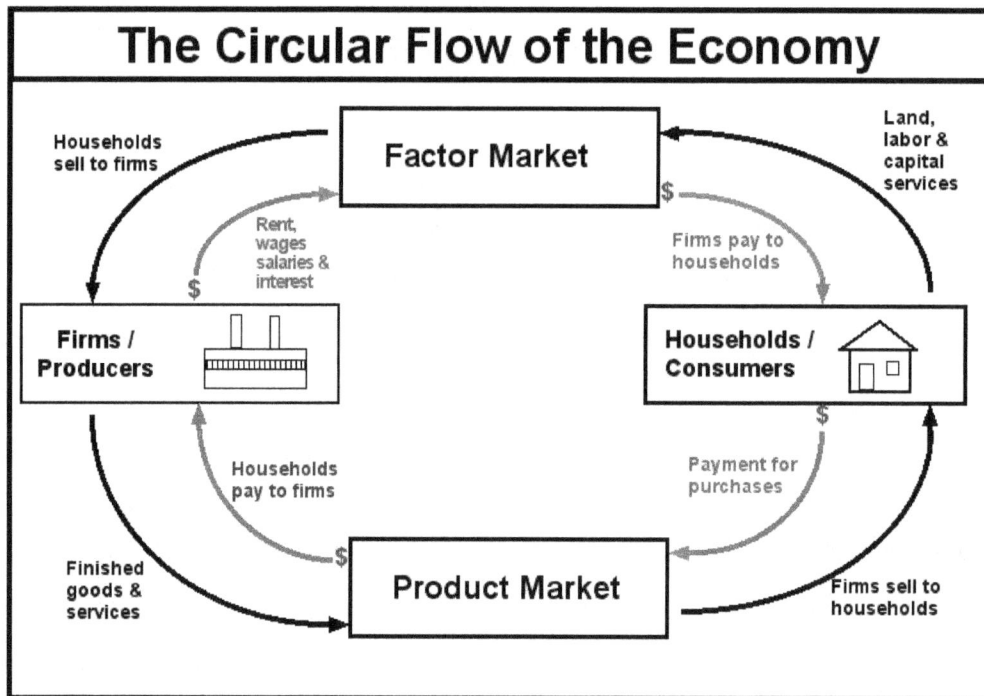

The Circular Flow Diagram shows the interdependence of economic systems. Businesses need consumers to buy their products, consumers need businesses to supply them with their desires and preferences, society needs doctors and in turn doctors need patients. Note however that this simple diagram does not show transactions between banks or investment companies, businesses with other businesses or foreign trade.

Market System Resolution vs. Alternatives

During most of the 20th century, there were two distinct competing systems: free-market and centrally directed. The Cold War during the 1950s-1990s is a clear example of these different ideologies contrasting and clashing with each other. Today, the contrast between different economic systems is less distinct. China and Russia now have many millionaires and Cuba may be on the cusp of radical change.

Economic Reasoning Questions 3.4

1. In the analytical diagram below draw in the ends of each arrow to indicate the circular flow of the economy.

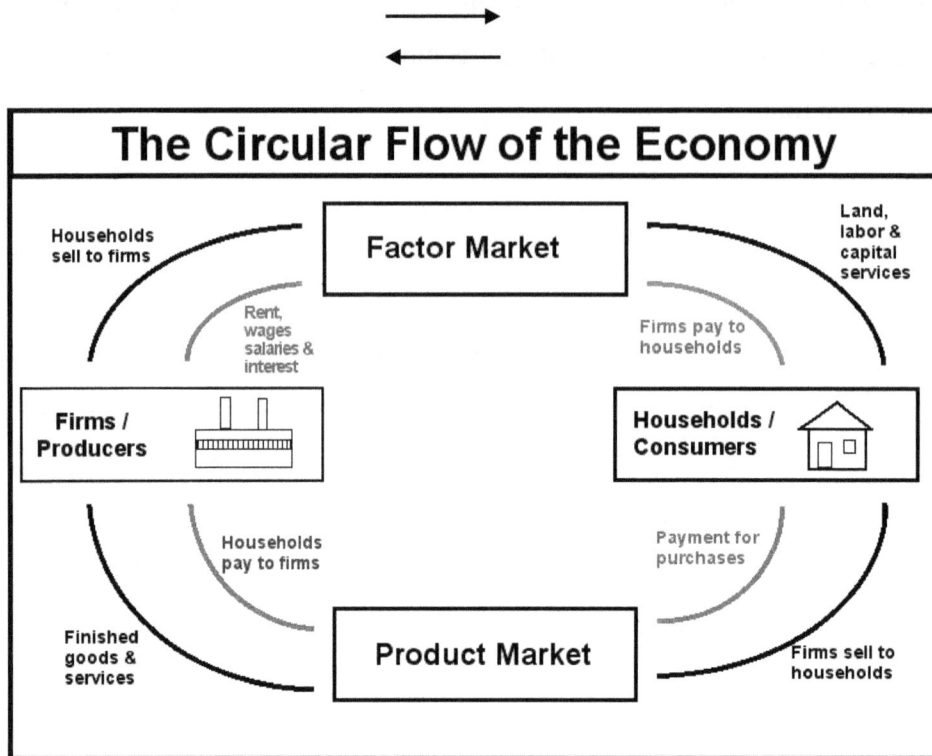

The Circular Flow of the Economy

Factor Market

Households
sell to firms

Land,
labor &
capital
services

Rent,
wages
salaries &
interest

Firms pay to
households

**Firms /
Producers**

**Households /
Consumers**

Households
pay to firms

Payment for
purchases

Finished
goods &
services

Product Market

Firms sell to
households

2. Market economies rely on the _____ motive of individuals to answer the three basic economic questions which are:

a. _____?

b. _____?

c. _____?

3. Lower prices provide incentives for producers to produce less/more and the consumers to buy less/more.

4. Higher prices provide incentives for producers to produce less/more and the consumers to buy less/more.

5. Consumers/households provide businesses/firms with

_____ , _____ and _____ services

in return for payment in the form of

_____ , _____ and _____ .

6. Businesses supply households with

_____ in return for _____ .

7. Which goods are <u>usually</u> sold in a factor market (F) or a product market (P)?

(there may be more than one answer, if you can support it)

a. Tractors _____   b. Automobiles _____

c. Computers _____   d. DVD's _____

e. Refrigerators _____   f. Diamonds _____

g. Televisions _____   h. Office buildings _____

i. Crude oil _____   j. Economics textbooks _____

k. A loaf of bread _____   l. A loaf of bread _____
(for sale in a supermarket)   (sold from a bakery to a local restaurant)

8. Give one example of when the following items would be sold in a factor market and one example when it would be sold in a product market

a. A microwave oven

Factor Market _____   Product Market_____

b. A computer

Factor Market _____   Product Market_____

c. A plumber's services

Factor Market _____   Product Market_____

SECTION 4

Supply, Demand, and Price in a Market System

R emember that the most important feature of a market economy is that resources are allocated by society's *voluntary* exchange of goods and services.

Each and every good or service has its price, and it is determined by the interaction of buyers, or *consumers*, and sellers, or *producers*.

The consumers' side of the market economy is called **demand** (usually referred to as **D**) and the sellers' side of the market economy is **supply** (usually referred to as **S**). The combined forces of supply and demand ultimately determine all prices of goods and services in a market economy.

Demand–The Consumers' Side of a Market Economy

Demand (**D**) is the relationship between how much of (or the *quantity* of) a good or service that consumers desire to purchase at any particular time, and the various *prices* that can exist for the good or service at that particular time.

This relationship is referred to at the *Law of Demand,* which states that the quantity demanded of a good or service varies *inversely* with its price. This means that the lower the price of the product, the bigger the quantity demanded for it; and conversely, the higher the price of the product, the smaller the quantity demanded for it.

Why does the Law of Demand prove to be basically true regarding consumers' behavior? There are two primary reasons, one is often referred to as the *substitution effect,* and the other is referred to as the *income effect*.

The *substitution effect* is the tendency of some consumers to switch to a less expensive alternative product, as that product good becomes more and more expensive. Think of a product you use regularly (pencils, printer paper, canned tomatoes, a favorite food product). You might be willing to pay different prices for this product, depending on how urgently you need it. But the higher the price is above what you usually expect to pay for that product, the more likely you will look for alternative products at a lower price to meet your needs at that particular time.

The *income effect* is the tendency of some consumers to not buy or buy less of a product, as that product good becomes more and more expensive. You might not buy that new computer or a new motorbike because your salary hasn't gone up as quickly as you had hoped or if the price of computer chips or gasoline has forced the prices of these products up.

You also might find evidence of the income effect regarding a product you use frequently and need a regular supply of. If you have lots of pencils and the school term is almost finished you might only buy many new pencils at a very low price (at an end-of-term 50%-off sale, perhaps). If the price of pencils was much higher than you prefer to pay, you might still buy pencils at a high price (if you had no pencils and you needed some for your economics test that day, for example), but you would probably buy fewer pencils at the higher price than you would at the lower price *most* of the time.

Lets say because of your cooking hobby, you frequently have use for canned chopped tomatoes, and you like to keep a small supply of a few cans in your cupboard. During your daily shopping you might have notices the price of canned tomatoes is not always the same. You may have also noticed that when the price drops to a lower level you seem to have the desire to buy several cans of tomatoes for your supply and when the prices seem a bit higher you don't seem to buy as much. If you wanted to gather some data to test as to whether the Law of Demand applied to your buying behavior, here you might record the number of cans of tomatoes you bought at different prices during the month. One way you could organize that data is on a *demand schedule*.

A **demand schedule** records the number of units of a product purchased for a given amount of time at each price level. For one person this is called an *individual demand schedule*, and for a larger group like a town or a city, it is called a *community demand schedule*. Your purchases of canned tomatoes over a one-month period might look something like the figure below.

Figure 4.1 -- Individual Demand Schedule for Canned Tomatoes

Price	Quantity Demanded
$1.00	5
$1.50	4
$2.00	3
$2.50	2
$3.00	1

If you were somehow able to get the data for all the individual canned tomato purchases in your entire town, you could organize the data into a community demand schedule that might look something like Figure 4.2.

61

Figure 4.2 -- Community Demand Schedule for Canned Tomatoes

Price	Quantity Demanded
$1.00	50,000
$1.50	40,000
$2.00	30,000
$2.50	20,000
$3.00	10,000

You could display this data as a visual model by plotting the number of cans bought at each different price level. This visual model is called a *demand curve*. A **demand curve** shows the inverse relationship between the price of the item and quantity demanded by the consumers of the item at each price level. Please note that the term "curve" is primarily used to name this diagram, not to describe its shape. While the shape of the line connecting the points plotted on the diagram may or may not have a curved shape, the diagram is still referred to a *demand curve*. The

FIGURE 4.3 -- Demand Curve

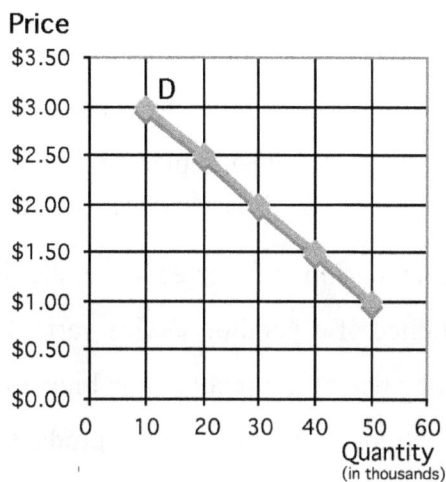

demand curve plotted for your community demand schedule data on cans of tomatoes purchased might look something like the figure above.

Economic Reasoning Questions 4.1

1. The law of demand states that:

a. As prices *decrease* the quantity of goods demanded will_____.

b. As prices *increase* the quantity of goods demanded will_____.

2. The demand curve demonstrates:

a. a relationship between two variables _____ and _____.

b. a slope down and to the right indicating these two variables have a(n)

_____ relationship.

3. In each of the following examples, indicate whether it represents the (S)ubstitution effect or (I)ncome effect on demand.

a. _____High beef prices means your family eats more chicken dishes.

b. _____Because of higher electricity prices Chris had to stop using his heater at night.

c. _____ When the price of rice goes up, Mary eats more potatoes.

d. _____ Higher gas prices means Joe cannot afford to drive as much as he used to.

e. _____ Super Cola prices go up so you buy Budget Cola instead.

Supply–The Producers' Side of a Market Economy

Supply (S) is the relationship between how much of (or the *quantity* of) a good or service that producers desire to make or *produce* at any particular time, at each possible price level at that particular time.

This relationship is referred to at the *Law of Supply,* which states that the quantity supplied of a good or service varies *directly* with its price. This means that the higher the price of the product, the bigger the quantity supplied will be for it; and conversely, the lower the price of the product, the smaller the quantity supplied will be for it.

Why does the Law of Supply prove to be basically true regarding Producers' behavior? Since the incentive to produce a product in a market economy is primarily profit, producers have more incentive at higher prices to produce more since they can receive more profits. Conversely producers have less incentive to produce goods and services at lower price levels because they will profit less.

Returning to the example of your canned tomato purchases, you might want to examine the Law of demand and the production behavior of a local company that produces canned tomatoes.

Perhaps the company shares with you its production numbers for the month. Just like your earlier examination of tomato purchases, you could organize that data in a *supply schedule*.

Figure 4.4 -- Community Supply Schedule

A **supply schedule** records the number of units of a product produced for a given amount of time at each price level. For one factory this is would be an

Price	Quantity Supplied
$1.00	10,000
$1.50	20,000
$2.00	30,000
$2.50	40,000
$3.00	50,000

individual supply schedule, and for a group of different producers in a particular area, it would be called a *community supply schedule*. If you were somehow able to get the data for all of the canned tomatoes purchased for your entire town, you could organize the data into a community demand schedule that might look something like Figure 4.4.

As with the demand curve, you can also display this data as a visual model by plotting the number of cans bought at each different price level. This visual model is called a *supply curve.*

Figure 4.5 -- Supply Curve

A **supply curve** shows the direct relationship between the price of the item and quantity supplied by the producers of the item at each price level. Again, the term "curve" refers to the name of the diagram rather than the shape of the line. The supply curve plotted for your data on cans of tomatoes produced might look something like the figure to the right.

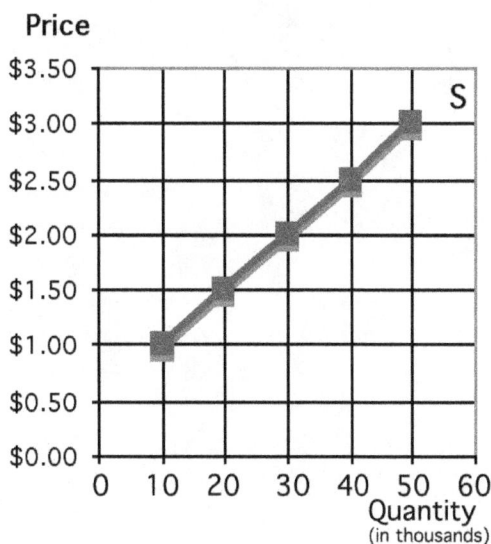

Economic Reasoning Questions 4.2

1. The law of supply states that:

a. As prices *decrease* the quantity of goods suppliers will provide will_____.

b. As prices *increase* the quantity of goods suppliers will provide will_____.

2. The supply curve demonstrates:

a. a relationship between two variables _____ and _____.

b. a slope up and to the right indicating these two variables have a(n) _____ relationship.

3. The incentive in a market economy that explains why suppliers will tend to produce more at higher prices and less at lower prices is called the _____ motive.

Where Supply and Demand Come Together.

It is important to remember that producers' behavior and consumers' behavior are determined independently. So producers like high prices and consumers like low prices. So how does a market economy ensure that we provide enough goods and services to meet the wants and needs of consumers, yet at the same time avoiding producing more goods and services that consumers are willing to purchase? The answer to this basic "What to produce?" Is determined by finding *market equilibrium.*

The **equilibrium price** is the point at which price of products offered by suppliers' equals the *quantity demanded* by purchasers.

The equilibrium point (**E**) is determined by plotting the supply curve and the demand curve for a particular graph and find the exact point where the two lines intersect. Find the equilibrium point on Figure 4.6

Figure 4.6 -- Market Equilibrium

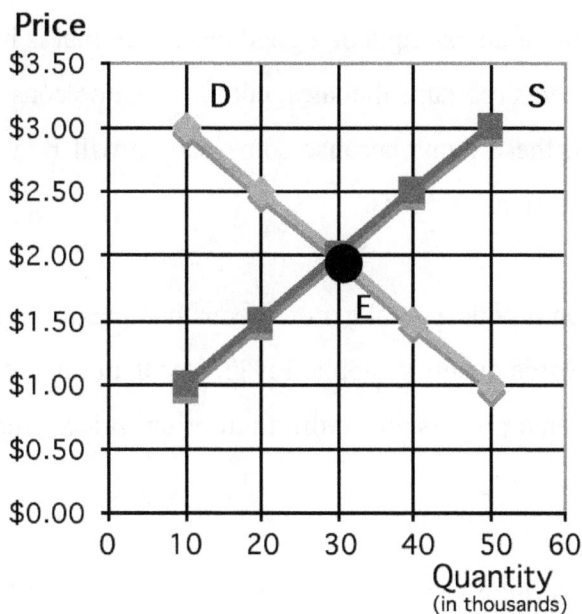

The Market Price - Equilibrium

Even though Supply and demand schedules/curves are determined independently, when they are combined together they determine the equilibrium price. The equilibrium price is the price at which the quantity of a good or service offered by suppliers is exactly equal to the quantity that is demanded by purchasers in a particular period of time.

That ideal balance of price and quantity is held in place by forces which economist Adam Smith referred to as "*the invisible hand*" in his book *The Wealth of Nations* in 1776. The invisible hand refers to the effects that *shortages* and *surpluses* have on prices.

A **shortage** occurs when not enough products are produced to meet the quantity demanded. This occurs when a price is below the equilibrium price. Simply put producers are not making enough of their goods to fulfill the desired purchases of the item. Usually shortages result in an increase in prices.

You can probably think of an example of a good or service that is highly desired but difficult to find in the stores (perhaps the latest computer game console). Usually this will push prices up for these items because some people will be willing to pay more to fulfill their personal wants or needs.

A **surplus** occurs when producers make more items than people want to buy at a particular price. In other words quantity supplied is greater than quantity demanded. Surpluses usually occur when a price is above the equilibrium price. Surpluses cause prices to decrease.

Think of your local clothing retailer putting items on sale after they have not sold for a certain amount of time. By lowering the price, the store will be increasing the chances that someone will be willing to purchase the item at the new lower price.

So the downward pressure on the equilibrium point caused by surpluses and the upward pressure on the equilibrium point caused by shortages, means that in a competitive market prices cannot stay above or below the equilibrium point for very long. The pressures created by competition for your business tend to push prices back down or up to the equilibrium point.

Up to this point, we have explored the interaction of the variables *price and quantity* regarding the behavior of producers and consumers. But there are additional factors that may influence all production or buying decisions at all possible price levels.

Economic Reasoning Exercise 4.3

1. A. use the supply and demand schedule provided below to create your own supply and demand curve for cups of coffee. Indicate the variables and units on the axis of each (you do not need to construct an entire grid).

Price	Quantity Demanded	Price	Quantity Supplied
$2	5	$2	1
$4	4	$4	2
$6	3	$6	3
$8	2	$8	4
$10	1	$10	5

Price|

0   Quantity

2. What is the equilibrium price and quantity for the curves you constructed?

    Price: _____ Quantity: _____

What Determines our Wants and Needs? -- Shifts in Demand.

There are five main *determinants*, or effects on demand: the preference, income, substitute, complement, and population effects. Each of these effects has the potential to influence change upon all price levels on the demand curve.

The **Preference Effect** is the influence on demand by individual consumer's liking or preference for specific goods or services. This effect includes likes and dislikes, fads and fashions, individual tastes, and good or bad publicity about a product (such as positive or negative health effects, for example).

If it became proven that eating lots tomatoes prevented all form of cancer, you might find that a change will occur in the demand schedule/curve you created earlier for the purchase of canned tomatoes in your town. The curve still exists because different individual are still willing to buy more or less at different price levels, however you would most likely see that more cans were being purchases at every price level. This would indicate an increase in demand (the whole curve shifted to the right).

The **Income Effect** recognizes that the amount of money held by individuals will influence what they buy. Without the ability to pay for a product, then of course the demand for that product cannot exist. In general, if incomes in a community increase (perhaps, due to the higher incomes generated by a strong economic cycle) then demand will generally increase as well. The opposite also tends to be the case; when incomes in a community decrease (perhaps due to a government tax increase) then demand will generally decrease.

A *substitute* is a product that can be used in place of another product. It is a lower priced alternative product that meets the consumers wants or needs as satisfactorily as the originally desired product. The **Substitute Effect** suggests that an increase in the price of a substitute increases the demand for other substitutes.

Perhaps you like to go out with your friends for pizza every Friday after class. You and your friends notice that recently the price of pizza has gone up considerably.

As a result, you and your friends decide to meet up for hamburgers instead the next week. This is an example of the substitute effect on our decisions as consumers. The increase in pizza prices has led to an increase in demand for hamburgers (a substitute product).

A *complement* is a product that is usually used with another product. The **Complement Effect** suggests that an increase in the price of a complement decreases the demand for other products and their complements.

For example, the use of your compact disc player requires the use of compact discs. The use of one product is usually used in combination with the other. If the price of one of these complements leads to a decision not to use the product in the future, then you will most likely not use the complementary product as much either. If consumer's music listening habits have led to their downloading most of their music from the Internet, they will be buying fewer CD's. The substitution effect suggests that there will be reduced demand for CD players in the future as well.

The **Population Effect** is the influence on demand by the number of people making purchases in the market area; mainly determined by the number of people living, working, and/or visiting in the market area. This increase might be from a more permanent change such as more new residents moving into town to take advantage of new housing or employment opportunities; or it might be temporary, such as the huge increase in visitors to cities hosting the Olympic games.

Economic Reasoning Questions 4.4

1. Which of the main determinants that effect demand is associated with each of the following examples?

a. A new portable music player model sells out in less than a week.

_____

b. Sales of home exercise equipment have seen a huge increase.

_____

c. After a new factory and large apartment building is constructed, the area sees increased sales in many goods and services. _____

d. Tea sales decreased when coffee prices decreased.

_____

e. Fewer new cars are sold during an economic recession.

_____

f. Sales of video tape players decline as videotapes become less popular.

_____

2. Will the following examples result in an increase or a decrease in the demand for hamburgers in a particular area. Indicate an increase "+" or decrease "-":

a. _____ The price of fried potatoes increases

b. _____ Average wage levels are up

c. _____ The area will host a popular spectator sporting event over the next
              month.

d. _____ The price for submarine sandwiches at a large chain restaurant go down.

e. _____ New research shows that fast food is far unhealthier than people
              previously thought.

f. _____ All fast food restaurants in the area decide to offer free soft drink refills.

What to Produce? -- Shifts in Supply.

As previously mentioned, the incentive to produce any product in a market economy is primarily the profit motive; therefore the cost to produce a product is very important to producers. Higher costs mean lower profits and lower costs mean higher profits. The most important effects, or determinates, on supply are those that influence the cost of production: resource costs (natural and human) and technology (capital).

An increase in resource prices such as the wages paid to workers or the prices of necessary natural resources will decrease the amounts of goods and services all producers are willing to supply at all price levels. The contrary is also true, a decrease in human resource prices or the prices of necessary natural resources will increase the amounts of goods and services all producers are willing to supply at all price levels.

Improvements in technology (equipment, software or information about new production processes) are considered capital improvements. Technological improvements increase efficiency, which usually leads to lower costs (or greater production at the same costs). Improvements in technology therefore usually lead to increases in supply.

Economic Reasoning Questions 4.5

1. The most important determinant of supply is _____.

2. Place a check next to each of the following examples that will have an effect on determining the *supply* of coffee.

a. _____ The price of tea decreases.

b. _____ New coffee roasting technology is developed.

c. _____ Many hurricanes last season has caused the price of coffee beans to rise.

d. _____ The demand for coffee increases

e. _____ The government places a new tax on all producers of coffee.

f. _____ New regulations increase the wages of field workers in coffee plantations.

Why Do Prices Change?

Changes in demand (D) and supply (S) cause prices to change. Prices, however, do <u>not</u> cause demand or supply to change. Differences in price only cause the *quantity* to change. The diagram below (4.7) demonstrates a change in price (moving from one point on the line to any other point) resulting in a change in quantity demanded and quantity supplied.

Figure 4.7a -- Differences in Price and Changes in Quantity Demanded

Here is how to demonstrate a change in price on a demand curve diagram.

Figure 4.7b -- Differences in Price and Changes in Quantity Supplied

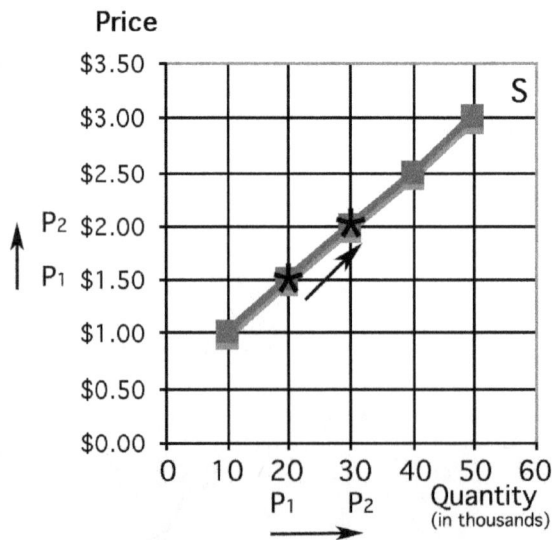

Likewise a change in price on the supply curve diagram. Note that in neither case did the lines change positions.

Indicating Shifts on the Demand Curve.

A change in demand is reflected by changes along the entire demand curve. In the case of demand, these changes are not caused by price, but by the *determinants* on demand: the preference, income, substitute, complement, and population effects. This means a change in the quantity of a good or service that would be purchased at each possible price. On the visual model, this would show a leftward shift of the entire curve (in case of a decrease in demand) or a rightward shift of the entire curve (in case of an increase in demand.) The figure below visually demonstrated an increase in demand (D).

Figure 4.8a -- An Increase in Demand　　　**Figure 4.8b -- A Decrease in Demand**

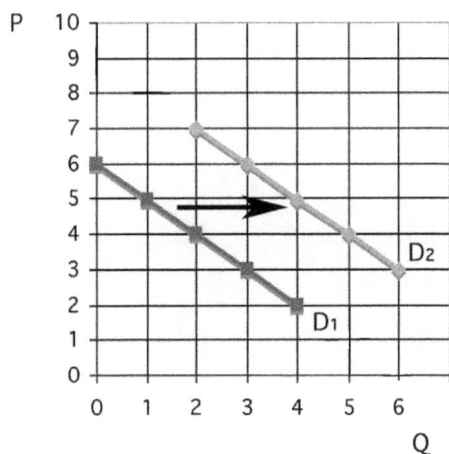

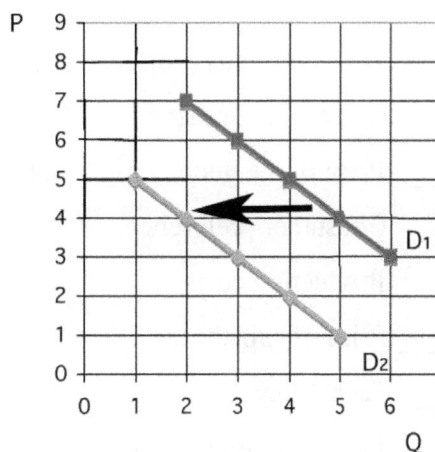

Compare this to figure 4.7a, which shows changes in the quantity demanded. These changes show movements by buyers along an existing demand curve. If you recall correctly, the things that cause demand to change (the determinants of demand) will not change the supply curve. So the result of an interaction between a new demand curve (D_2) and an unchanged supply curve (S) will be a new equilibrium price (E_2) in the short run.

Figure 4.9 -- Shift in Demand with Supply remaining the same

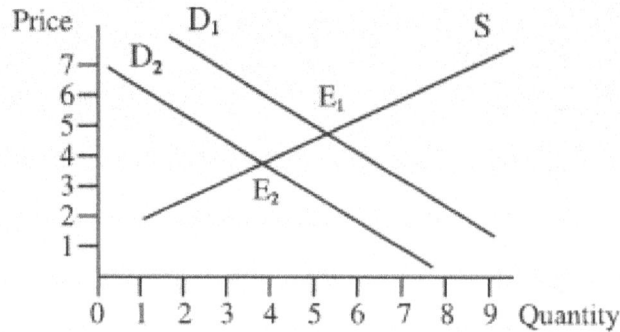

This figure demonstrates a decrease in demand (D$_2$), which both decreases the equilibrium price (from 5 to 4) and decreases the quantity supplied (also from 5 to 4) in the short term.

Economic Reasoning Questions 4.6

1. Place a check next to each of the following that can cause demand (and therefore the demand curve) to increase or decrease.

a. _____ Consumers' income

b. _____ Price of the good being purchased

c. _____ Consumer preferences

d. _____ Production costs

e. _____ Price of substitutes

f. _____ Technology

g. _____ Price of complements

h. _____ Population

i. _____ Cost of resources for suppliers

Changes in the Supply Curve

A change in supply is reflected by changes along the entire supply curve. This means a change in the quantity of a good or service that would be offered for sale at each possible price. On the visual model this would show a leftward shift of the entire curve (in case of a decrease in supply) or a rightward shift of the entire curve (in case of an increase in supply.) The figures below visually demonstrate a increase and decrease in supply (S).

Figure 4.11a -- Increase in Supply   **Figure 4.11b -- Decrease in Supply**

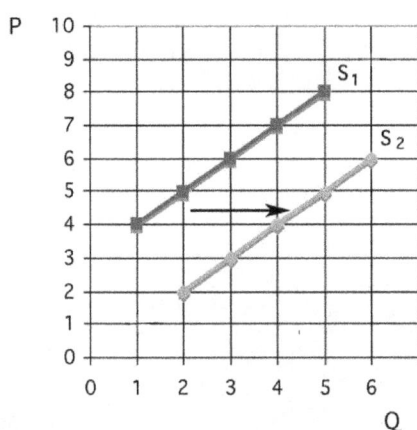

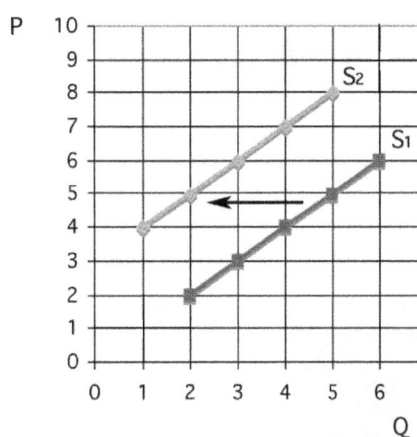

Again, compare this to figure 4.7b, which show changes in the quantity supplied. These changes show movements by buyers along existing supply curves. An increase in supply, (caused by changes in production costs) however, results in a new curve (S_2). Demand will remain unchanged, but the new location of the supply curve will result in the raising of the equilibrium price and a decrease in the quantity demanded in the short term.

Examine figure 4.12, which demonstrates a change in the supply curve and the equilibrium price and quantity even though demand remains unchanged.

Figure 4.12 - Shift in Supply with Demand remaining the same

The result of the reduction in supply in this case is a higher equilibrium price but a lower quantity demanded.

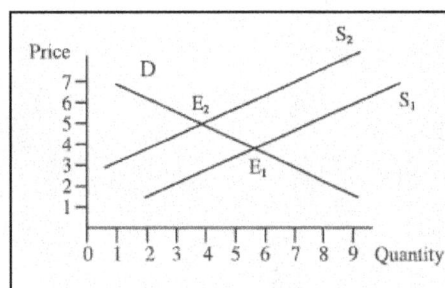

Economic Reasoning Questions 4.6

1. Place a check next to each of the following that can cause supply (and therefore the supply curve) to increase or decrease.

a. _____ Consumer Income

b. _____ Producers' labor costs

c. _____ Final price of the good being produced

d. _____ Suppliers' production costs

e. _____ Population

f. _____ Technology

g. _____ Complements

h. _____ Cost of resources

SECTION FIVE

The Concept of Price Elasticity

Supply, demand and market equilibrium are simple and understandable models for explaining how goods and services are priced in a market economy. But as you might expect of a model, reality is usually more complicated. In this section we will discuss the consumer's role in the economy and introduce another economic concept that influences market prices, price *elasticity*.

The Consumer and Income

People earn income in different ways. As we discussed in Section Three, households receive different forms of factor payments for the land, labor and capital resources they sell to businesses in the factor market. For their *labor* services households receive **wages** and/or **salaries**, for any *land* use households receive **rent**, and for the use of their *financial capital* households receive *interest*. A fourth factor payment that we have not previously discussed is **profits**, which is the factor payment for **entrepreneurship**. An entrepreneur is a person (or firm) who brings together the necessary factors of production to create a new product or process to meet an existing unfulfilled demand. Entrepreneurship does entail an element of risk, and in return for their efforts entrepreneurs hope to receive payment in the form of profits. In the case of corporate entrepreneurship it is the owners of the corporation (often this would be the shareholders) who hope to share these profits in the form of *dividends*.

For most households the main source of their income is in the form of wages and salaries paid to them for their **labor**. The price of labor, like any other resource in a market economy is determined primarily through *supply* and *demand*.

Labor Supply and Demand

The demand for labor is what economists call a **derived demand**. A derived demand for one good or service occurs as a result of demand for a different good or service. For example, the demand for oil leads to a derived demand for oil drilling (because if the oil is to be consumed it first has to be extracted by oil drillers).

The amount of capital used by business affects the demand for labor. Capital can act as both a substitute and a complement to labor. If the capital results in the elimination of a job (like a robot replacing an assembly line worker, or online video lectures replacing your economics teacher) then it is a substitute and decreases the demand for labor. If new capital requires additional skilled labor to operate and/or maintain the new equipment, then it is a compliment and increases demand for labor.

The *supply* of labor reflects the number of people who have the needed skills and want to work. The amount people earn from their wages and salaries are determined by the interaction of labor supply and demand.

Figure 5.1

Effect on Wages of an Increase in Labor Supply and Demand

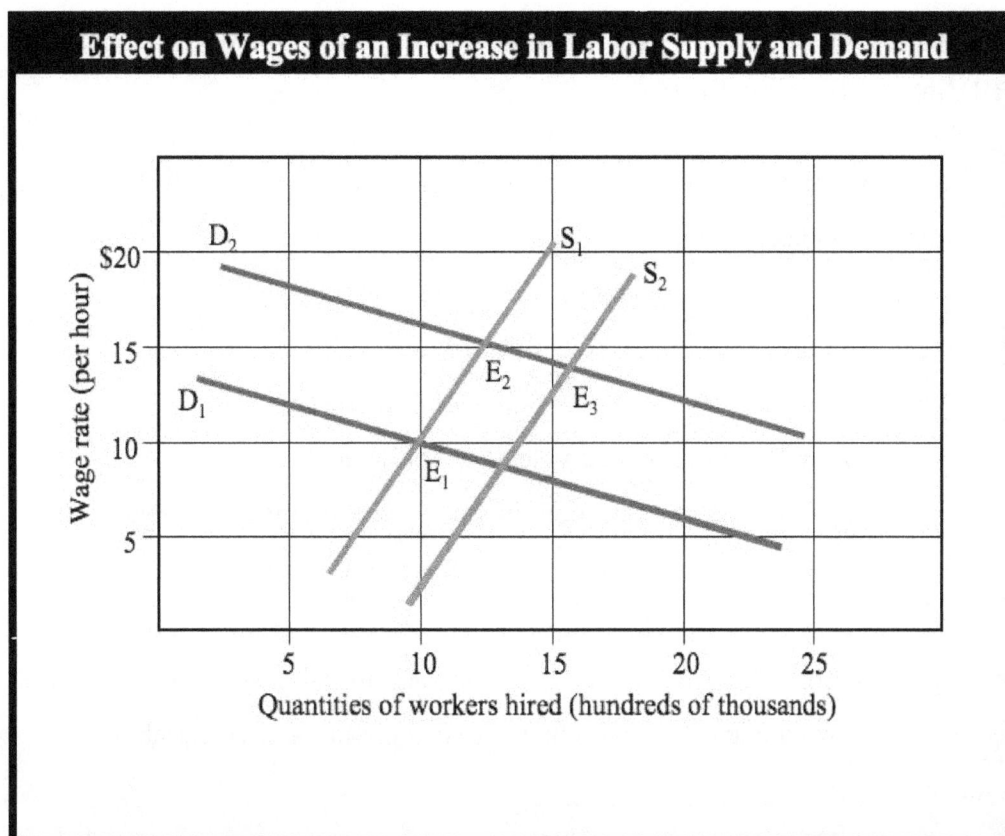

The explosive growth of the number of Internet users leads to an increase in demand for company and product websites. This in turn leads to an increase in demand for web site designers (another example of *derived demand*). In figure 5.1 above, the wages for web site designers is determined by the interaction of supply (S_1) and demand (D_1) for workers with the necessary skills. As demand for web site designers increased from D_1 to D_2, wages increased from $10 per hour ($E_1$) to $15 dollars per hour ($E_2$). These higher wages attracted the attention of people seeking work (or willing to change their jobs) who would now be willing to do web site design at the new wage level. This new larger pool of potential workers causes an increase in the supply (S_2) of labor. This shift in supply creates yet another equilibrium price and represents a decline in wages to $13 per hour. ($E_3$). This is how a market system allocates labor to occupations where it is most needed and therefore most highly valued.

Economic Reasoning Questions 5.1

1. Indicate whether each of the following factor payments come in the form of wages (W), rent (R), interest (I), or profits (P).

a. _____ Every month the bank pays you a small percentage of the value of the money you keep there.

b. _____ Money received from the sale of some farmland.

c. _____ Salary paid to a firm's chief executive officer (CEO).

d. _____ Weekly paycheck for a worker at a fast food restaurant.

e. _____ Mega Corporation pays out a dividend to its shareholders.

f. _____ Money received renting out a room in your house to university students.

g. _____ A corporation pays for the use of money borrowed from a bank's depositors.

2. If increasing the amount of capital decreases the demand for labor (such as replacing your classrooms and teachers with interactive computer and video labs), then labor and capital are _____.

3. If increasing the amount of capital increases the demand for labor (such as adding a new piece of equipment that needs additional people to operate and maintain), then labor and capital are _____.

Rent and Rent-Type Earnings

As mentioned in the introduction to this section, **rent** is the factor payment for the use of *land*. Land is a rather special resource however in that the supply of land is mostly *fixed*. As the famous piece of financial advice puts it, *"Buy land, because God isn't making any more of it."* This is significant because if the supply of land is fixed, it means that rent is almost entirely determined by demand. If there is a big demand for land in a certain location (such as in a city center or a beautiful beach), rent is likely to be very high. Conversely, if demand for land in a location is small (such as a rural area or a dangerous neighborhood), the rent payment for use of the land will likely be low. Unlike other factors, the supply of land cannot adjust to price changes because it is relatively fixed.

Figure 5.2 demonstrates this concept in the form of a supply and demand curve. The supply of rent (S_1) is vertical because the quantity of land is fixed and does not change with the price of using it (rent). The S_2 curve shows a more familiar supply curve for a different product (say canned tomatoes or automobile insurance). Compare the effects of an increase in demand on rent verses the other product. The increase in price for the other product (x) is fairly small compared with the increased price (rent) for the use of land (y).

Figure 5.2

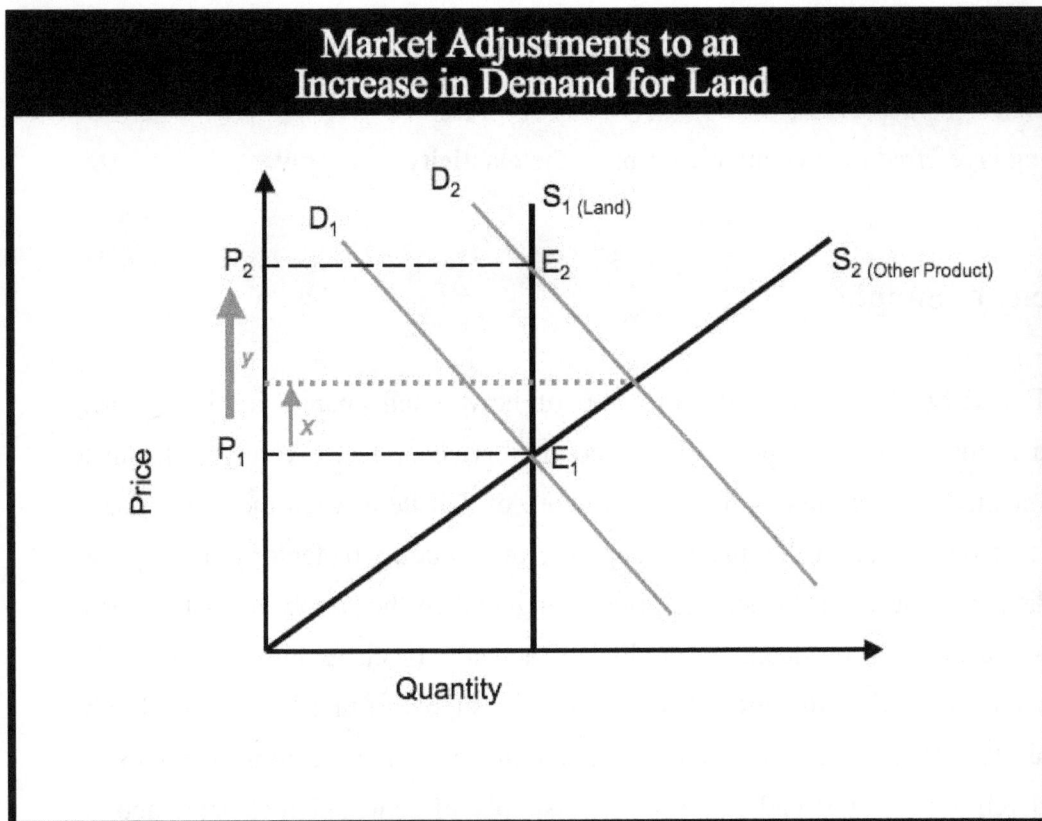

Rent-type earnings can sometimes be found in the form of wages and salaries. For most occupations the types of skills required are abundant enough that the supply of workers attracted by higher wages can accommodate the increased demand (such as the S_2 curve in figure 5.2 above). However if some sort of unique talent is required (such as the ability to sell out a rock concert, or draw moviegoers to see a film, or hit many home runs), the supply of people with that ability is very limited. Certainly many of us would love to be rock stars, movie stars or baseball heroes and would be very willing to accept lower wages than are currently being offered to such types, but unfortunately we to not have the necessary characteristics to perform these jobs. Therefore, the supply of baseball stars, for example is fairly limited and the supply curve for such labor would more closely resemble S_1 rather than S_2 on figure 5.2. This explains why actors and singers who can draw large audiences earn such huge salaries. The difference in the supply curves for different types if labor is explained in the economic concept known as *elasticity*.

Price Elasticity of Supply and Demand

Price elasticity is a very important element in understanding the behavior of producers and consumers. The example of the supply of labor that we have been discussing is referred to in economic terms as the **elasticity of supply**.

Elasticity of Supply

Elasticity of Supply is the measure of how much change in the quantity supplied is made when the price of that good, service or factor changes. Inelastic supply means that it is impossible to make more of that item when there is a rise in the price of that good. If the quantity supplied of a product or factor (such as low-skilled labor) changes a lot when the price changes, then the supply of that factor is said to be **elastic**. If the quantity supplied of a factor (such as high-skilled labor) changes very little when the price changes, then the supply of that factor is said to be **inelastic**. We reviewed an example of this phenomenon in the previous discussion of rent and rent-type wages and salaries. The supply of rent and rock star labor is inelastic; meaning it is relatively fixed and therefore forms a nearly vertical line on the supply curve, as is the case for S_1 below. Where the line is vertical and therefore supply is absolutely fixed, this is said to be **perfectly inelastic**.

Economic Reasoning Questions 5.2

1. The amount of rent one must pay for the use of land depends almost exclusively on demand because the supply of land is mainly _____ or _____.

2. The necessary skills demanded for some types of jobs like baseball stars can only be performed by a very few people, therefore wages for this type of labor more closely resemble _____.

Elasticity of Demand

Consumers are faced with spending choices every day. While the law of demand states that consumers tend to buy less of a good at higher prices, it does not explain the *degree* to which price changes affect the quantity demanded. The concept of elasticity can also be used to explain the degree of changes in the quantity demanded.

A good example of difference in the degree of relation of price to quantity could be found in a study of data on cigarette sales. A look at demand for cigarettes from different age groups would likely show that an increase in the price if cigarettes would probably cause a large drop in the quantity of cigarettes demanded by consumers in the 18 to 25 age group. However, the data would probably show a much smaller drop in quantity demanded by consumers aged 30 to 40. In economic terms, this could be described that the demand for cigarettes in the younger age group is more elastic than demand for cigarettes in the older group. Why is this the case? Well, there are several determinants of elasticity, but in the case of cigarettes it probably involves the addictive nature of nicotine, an ingredient found in cigarettes. For the young, cigarettes might be considered a luxury or a fashionable product. After years of use however, older

Economics in Action:
Many governments around the world have put the economic concepts of *demand* and *elasticity* to work for policy goals. The heavy taxation of tobacco products has been implemented in many markets in part to provide a disincentive for younger people to start smoking (and the relatively elastic nature of cigarette demand by younger smokers suggests this might be effective!). Secondly, the revenue generated by such taxes has been put to use for anti-smoking advertising campaigns or funding medical care for smoking related illnesses.

smokers might have more difficulty quitting, even after considerable price increases. In their case cigarettes might be considered more of a necessity.

On the demand curve, like the supply curve, elasticity is reflected in the slope of the line representing demand. In the case of normal goods, when a product has a large change in quantity demanded after a small change in the price of that good (such as cigarettes with younger consumers), it is said to be more elastic, or **relatively elastic** (see D_1 in figure 5.3 below). When a product has a small change in quantity demanded even after a significant change in the price of that good (such as cigarettes with older consumers), it is said to be less elastic, or **relatively inelastic** (see D_2). At the extreme, when changes in price result in no changes in the quantity demanded, the demand curve would be straight up and down (see D_3). At the opposite extreme, **perfectly elastic** is when a rise in the price would reduce quantity demanded to zero (see D_4).

Figure 5.3

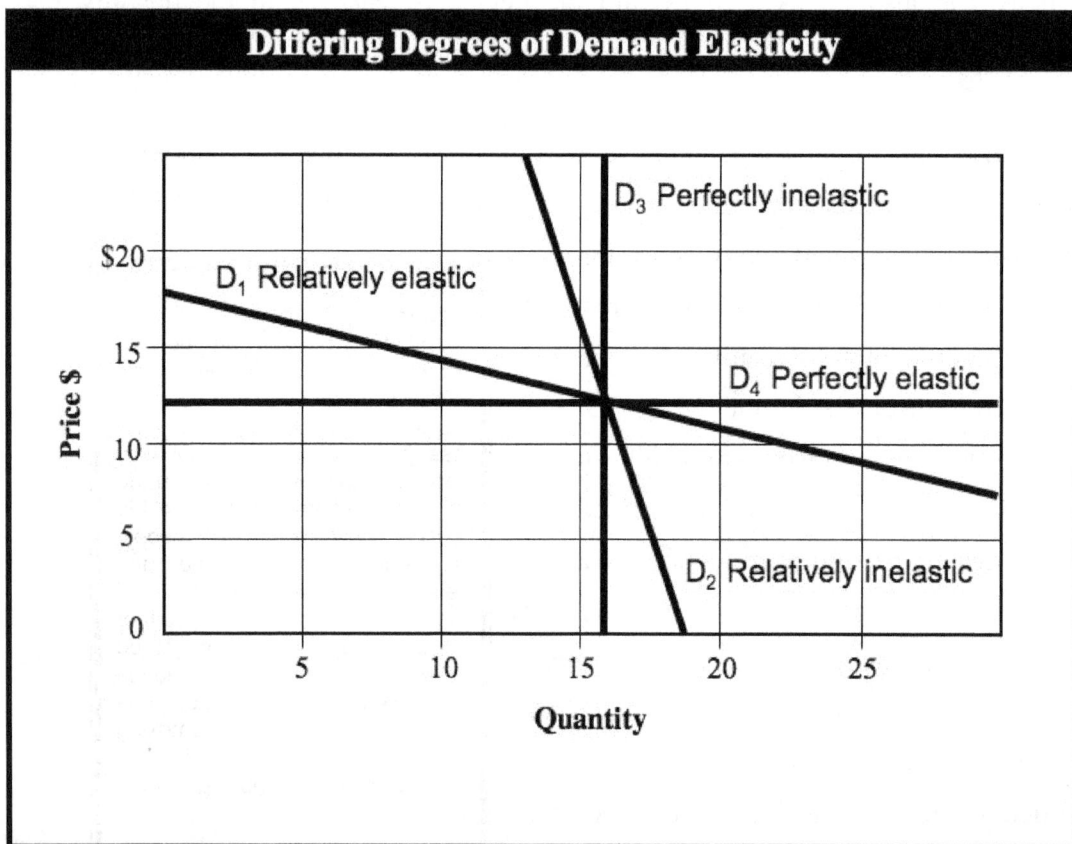

Differing Degrees of Demand Elasticity

What makes some products more elastic than others? The first determinant of elasticity is whether the products would be considered *luxuries or necessities,* or as we discussed in Section One, *wants or needs.* A **necessity** (or a *need*) is a product that is considered essential to a person's well being, such as electricity, insulin for diabetics, or motor oil for car owners. Necessities are inelastic because people need to buy them no matter the price. Salt is a good example of a necessity that is required by the human body. Salt also has few close substitutes. If the price of salt were to double in price, there would probably be little decrease in the quantity demanded.

Luxuries (or *wants*) however, are products we might like to have (such as a tickets to a concert, a particular brand of athletic shoes, or a vacation to Hawaii) but they are not considered essential in daily life. Luxuries are elastic because people don't need to buy them.

As mentioned above, a related determinant of elasticity is the availability of close **substitutes**. As we discussed in the previous section, substitutes are products that are similar or that serve the same function (fulfilling the consumer's wants and needs). Imagine going of to a soft drink machine and the brand and type of beverage you usually prefer is 20% higher than all the other drinks available. It would be fairly simple for you to chose a different beverage and avoid the extra cost. Products that have many close substitutes have high elasticity because it is relatively easy for consumers to switch to an alternative product to avoid paying a higher price.

Another determinant of elasticity related to substitutes is the **time horizon,** or the length of the production run of the product. Goods tend to be more elastic after a long time period because consumers will eventually find a substitute.

Economic Reasoning Questions 5.3

1. For both supply and demand, elasticity refers to the degree to which

_____ reacts to changes in _____.

2. Indicate whether the demand for each of the following is elastic (E) or inelastic (I)

a. _____ Yachts

b. _____ Soap

c. _____ Gasoline

d. _____ Dinoco brand gasoline

e. _____ A Rolls Royce automobile

f. _____ Electricity

g. _____ Cheeseburgers

2a. If there are very few substitutes for a product (such as tickets to a big sports event that is not on television) then the demand for that product will likely be

_____.

2b. However if there are sufficient substitutes available (say the game is broadcast on television and streaming over the internet), demand will likely be

_____.

Measuring the Elasticity of Demand

Since price elasticity is such an important characteristic for understanding spending decisions by consumers and pricing decisions by producers, it is useful to have a measurement of elasticity. One way to measure elasticity of demand is to calculate the **elasticity ratio** by dividing the percentage change in quantity demanded by the percentage change in price.

$$\textbf{Elasticity Ratio} = \frac{\textbf{\% change in quantity demanded (Q)}}{\textbf{\% change in price (P)}}$$

If the elasticity ratio is greater than 1 it is said to be elastic. If the elasticity ratio is less than 1 it is said to be inelastic. An elasticity ratio of exactly one is called **unitary elasticity**. The higher the elasticity, the more shallow the slope of the demand curve will be. The lower the inelasticity, the steeper the slope of the demand curve will be.

Elasticity ratio < 1 -- Elastic
Elasticity ratio > 1 -- Inelastic
Elasticity ratio = 1 -- Unitary Elasticity

Let's say that a 10% price increase for Brand X Cola results in 13% drop in quantity demanded.

$$\text{Elasticity Ratio for Brand X Cola} = \frac{\text{\% change in Q}}{\text{\% change in P}} = \frac{13\%}{10\%} = 1.40$$

This calculates an elasticity ratio of 1.40 which is greater than 1 and therefore relatively elastic. Let's compare this with another example. Let's say that due to a rise in production costs, the price of insulin increases 10%. Now not that many people need insulin, but for those people with diabetes, insulin provides the means for a manageable life. Furthermore there are virtually no substitutes for insulin. Therefore despite the 10% increase in price, we see only a 1% reduction in quantity demanded

$$\text{Elasticity Ratio for Insulin} = \frac{\text{\% change in Q}}{\text{\% change in P}} = \frac{1\%}{10\%} = 0.1$$

This calculates an elasticity ratio of 0.1, which is considerably less than 1 and therefore highly inelastic.

Economic Reasoning Questions 5.4

1. Compute the elasticity ratio for the following cases of changes in price (P) and quantity (Q). Then indicate the type of elasticity of each: relatively elastic (RE), unitary elastic (UE), relatively inelastic (RI), and perfectly inelastic (PI). Then give an example of a product that would likely demonstrate that characeristic.

a. P increases 25% and Q decreases 50% ER= _____ Type_____

    An example might be _____

b. P decreases 50% and Q decreases 50% ER= _____ Type_____

    An example might be _____

c. P decreases 10% and Q decreases 10% ER= _____ Type_____

    An example might be _____

d. P decreases 15% and Q doesn't change ER= _____ Type_____

    An example might be _____

e. P increases 1% and Q falls to zero ER= _____ Type_____

    An example might be _____

Afterword

The authors hope that you found this book useful, and that you are well on your way towards a sound understanding of economic fundamentals.

There are of course many other important economic concepts to study. Hopefully your use of this book has provided you with a firm foundation for further study.

We wish you good luck in your future study of microeconomics, macroeconomics, and/or international economics.

For those of you who would like to check your work relating to the economic reasoning questions, a free supplement will be made available for download at http://mselzer.tripod.com/book/ . The supplement contains answers and examples for all the exercises in this book.

Notes:

www.ingramcontent.com/pod-product-compliance
Lightning Source LLC
Chambersburg PA
CBHW081408200326

41518CB00013B/2274